*SCOTTISH*
*STEAM*
*TODAY*

by the same author

*Holiday Cruising in Ireland*

*Railways Revived*

*Waterways Restored*

*Your Book of Canals*

*The Archaeology of Canals*

*The Archaeology of Railways*

*Your Book of Steam Railway Preservation*

*The Archaeology of the Transport Revolution 1750 – 1850*

*Transport in Scotland through the Ages*

*The Victorian Railway and How It Evolved*

# SCOTTISH STEAM TODAY

by
P J G RANSOM

RICHARD DREW
PUBLISHING

GLASGOW

First published in 1989 by
Richard Drew Publishing Ltd
6 Clairmont Gardens
Glasgow G3 7LW
Scotland

British Library Cataloguing in Publication Data
Ransom, P J G (Philip John Greer), 1935-
   Scottish steam today.
   1. Scotland, Steam engines, history
   I. Title
   621.1′09411

   ISBN 0-86267-251-1 (Hardback)

   ISBN 0-86267-252-X (Paperback)

Designed by James W Murray

Printed and bound by
Eagle Press plc, Blantyre, Scotland

# CONTENTS

# $S$ *TEAM*
# $P$ *AST*
# $A$ *ND*
# $P$ *RESENT*

*M c A N D R E W*

*Not but they're ceevil on the Board. Ye'll hear Sir Kenneth say:*
*'Good morrn, McAndrew! Back again? An' how's your bilge to-day?'*
*Miscallin' technicalities but handin' me my chair*
*To drink Madeira wi' three Earls – the auld Fleet Engineer*
*That started as a boiler-whelp – when steam and he were low.*
*I mind the time we used to serve a broken pipe wi' tow!*
*Ten pound was all the pressure then – Eh! Eh! – a man wad drive;*
*An' here, our workin' gauges give one hunder sixty-five!*
From *McAndrew's Hymn* by Rudyard Kipling

$I$t was no coincidence that Kipling's 'auld Fleet Engineer', philosophising through a sleepless night beside his engines, was a Scot. Much pioneering work on steam boats had been done in Scotland, and they first saw intensive use on the Clyde in the second decade of the nineteenth century. This had given Scots engineers a head start which they had never lost. By 1893, when the poem was written, Scottish ships' engineers were pre-eminent.

So was steam. Scotland prospered on steam-powered industry, and on steam-powered transport by land and sea. As Summerlee Heritage Trust reminds us, the national dress was not so much the kilt as the boiler suit. Steam trains and steam ships were particularly conspicuous: operating in public, frequently encountered, large, and noisy, yet never offensive. Rather they were friendly, helpful and symbolic of prosperity.

Eventually more efficient and less conspicuous forms of power took over. Today, steam power is conspicuous only by its absence. Scottish

Everyone travelled by steam train: Glasgow Central on Fair Saturday.

T. & R. ANNAN & SONS LTD

steam today? What steam? – people enquired, on learning that I was writing a book about it. Yet research for it produced more and more locations at which steam transport, steam power or relics of steam are to be found. This is I believe the first attempt to produce a comprehensive guide, and the criterion for inclusion is accessibility by the public. But this is more, I hope, than a simple tourist guide. I have endeavoured not only to describe what is where, but to say how it comes to be there, what is its significance, where it fits into the overall picture. So far as opening dates and times are concerned, it is possible in a book like this to give only general guidance: precise dates and times vary annually and are best sought from operators themselves, whose addresses appear as an appendix.

I concentrate on full-size trains, ships and engines. Miniatures and models are mentioned, but only to a limited extent. Live steam models, in particular, sometimes enable us to perpetuate in miniature experiences no longer possible in full size. And the dividing line between full size and miniature is in any case blurred. Is the Mull railway miniature or narrow gauge?

This is not a 'rivet-counting' book. Technical details of steam ships and boats appear in the Steam Boat Association's publication *Steamboats and Steamships of the British Isles*, details of locomotives at each location appear in *Railways Restored*, and in stock books and the like published by individual operating groups. There are some suggestions for further reading at the end of the book.

With space limited, I have had to assume some degree of technical understanding on the part of the reader, though the book will not, I hope, prove incomprehensible to anyone. On the other hand, some

The Broomielaw, Glasgow, in 1894, with plenty of steamships on the move. *Cluthas* like the one in the left foreground provided what was in effect a water bus service.

attempt to outline the rise and decline of steam power in Scotland is essential, despite the risk of superficiality, so that what survives may be put into context, and this attempt follows.

*U*se of steam as a source of power originated from seventeenth and eighteenth century investigations into atmospheric pressure. The first practical application of steam was Thomas Newcomen's atmospheric pump for mine drainage – the first was built in 1712, and the first in Scotland installed about 1719. In operation, steam from a boiler was condensed beneath a piston in a large vertical open-topped cylinder: this created a partial vacuum so that atmospheric pressure drove the piston downwards. It was connected to one end of a vast rocking beam, to the other end of which was connected the pump rod, rising as the piston fell. Once the piston was at the bottom of its stroke, steam was admitted beneath it so that the weight of the pump rod caused it to rise; and then water was injected to condense the steam, and so on.

James Watt, a native of Greenock who became instrument maker to Glasgow University, realised that injecting water into the cylinder at the end of each stroke meant alternately cooling and heating the cylinder and so was terribly inefficient. In 1769 he patented his separate condenser, which condensed the steam in a chamber separate from the cylinder and so enabled the cylinder itself to be kept hot. Initial development work was done at Kinneil House, Bo'ness (where Watt's workshop still exists), but in 1774 Watt entered into a long-lasting and successful partnership with Matthew Boulton in Birmingham. The separate condenser and improved manufacturing techniques enabled the partnership to build pumps with both ends of the cylinder closed, and steam at a pressure a little above atmospheric was used to propel the piston to and fro, the used steam still being condensed. Replacing the pump rod by a connecting rod attached to a crank or similar device produced a steam engine with rotary motion.

Watt preferred to perfect the stationary engine rather than try to adapt it to power steam ships or vehicles; and his patent, which lasted until 1800, meant that much of the early work on these was done abroad, in France and the USA. John Fitch operated a steamboat on the Delaware River during 1790 and seems to have been defeated mainly by the reluctance of passengers to travel on it. The pioneering work of William Symington in Scotland is described in chapter ten. Robert Fulton in 1807 was the first to make a commercial success of operating a steam boat, with his *Clermont* on the Hudson River, driven by an engine supplied by Boulton, Watt & Co., successor to the Boulton & Watt partnership. Henry Bell emulated him in 1812 when his *Comet* on the Clyde became the first steam boat to operate a service outside North America.

Once Bell had shown the way, many rushed to follow him. Steam ships and boats were introduced on routes that were at first coastal, then cross-channel, and eventually, from the 1830s, ocean-going. Building steam ships developed into a prominent industry, particularly on the Clyde. In marine engines, from *Clermont* onwards, the cylinder at first remained upright but the overhead beam was replaced by side levers low down to which the piston was connected by rods. Propulsion was by paddle wheels; later the cylinder position changed by stages to become near-horizontal with drive direct on to the paddle shaft. Development of satisfactory screw propellers in the late 1840s led to engines with cylinders inverted above a crankshaft in line with the propeller shaft. Steam pressures gradually increased (to an extent at which McAndrew marvelled) and in compound engines steam from a first, high pressure, cylinder was re-used in a second at low pressure. The principle was later extended to triple and quadruple expansion engines with steam passing successively through three or four cylinders before being condensed.

Towards the end of the eighteenth century Cornishman Richard Trevithick had been one of many engineers who attempted to evade Watt's patent, and had realised he could eliminate the condenser by using 'strong steam' at pressures of around 50 lbs per sq. in. and exhausting into the air. More important, this enabled boiler and engine to be made very compact by contemporary standards: small enough to drive a vehicle. Trevithick experimented with road steam carriages, and in 1803 built the first workable railway locomotive. There had been simple railways, using horses and gravity for motive power, for many decades. The breakthrough, however, came in 1829 when George Stephenson, his son Robert and Henry Booth designed the locomotive *Rocket*, for the Liverpool & Manchester Railway, with a multi-tubular boiler which generated enough steam for it to run fast and far. Railways operated by such locomotives were both quicker and cheaper than horse-drawn road coaches, and throughout the rest of the century a railway system was built throughout most of Britain. Railways were built and operated by separate companies; successive amalgamations brought most Scottish railways into one or other of five large companies (Caledonian, North British, Glasgow & South Western, Highland, and Great North of Scotland). By the turn of the century in Scotland everyone travelling, or sending goods, for more than a few miles was almost certain to use steam train or steam ship.

So, too, steam engines were providing power in factories, mines and mills. Eighteenth-century beam engines were vast, but smaller ones had been developed, and so had many other steam-engine layouts intended to achieve compactness. One of the most popular was the horizontal engine, with horizontal cylinder(s) and direct drive on to a crankshaft. The steam turbine was developed in 1884 by the Hon. C. F. Parsons to drive dynamos, and successfully adopted for marine use the following decade.

'Portable' engines, largely for agricultural use, had been produced in the 1840s: boiler, cylinders and crankshaft were mounted together on wheels, to be moved by horse or hand to wherever they were needed. From these evolved self-propelled traction engines, steam rollers, road locomotives and, eventually, steam wagons. Attempts to build and operate road steam carriages in the early part of the nineteenth century had been eclipsed by steam railways, and subsequent attempts, made in Scotland and elsewhere in Britain, were hampered by restrictive roads legislation. For the same reason development of internal combustion engined vehicles towards the end of the century took place largely abroad; but such developments encouraged also construction of light steam cars. After restrictions were eased in Britain, steam cars remained competitive with motor into the 1920s; heavy steam road vehicles lasted until the 1940s and 50s.

By the end of the First World War motor lorries, motor buses and motor cars had developed sufficiently to offer travellers and traders transport that was cheaper, quicker and more convenient than steam railways. By the mid-1930s air travel was competitive with both railways and coastal shipping. At the grouping of 1923, Scottish railway companies had been amalgamated either into the new London, Midland & Scottish Railway (Caledonian, Highland and G & SW) or the new London & North Eastern Railway (North British, GNSR), but in 1948 these were nationalized and a Scottish Region of British Railways set up. Latterly it has been marketed as ScotRail. Numerous stations and lines were closed in the 1930s, and far more in the 1950s and 60s. Now most railways are operated by diesel or electric power: British Rail last operated its own steam locomotives in Scotland in 1967, or perhaps 1968, for steam locomotives from North West England seem to have continued to work into Scotland after Scottish-based locomotives had been withdrawn. Steam locomotives survived in industrial use, and particularly in coal mining, into the 1980s.

Afloat, small motor vessels were being built in the second decade of this century, and ever larger ones in the decades which followed. In mirror image of this, construction and use of steam ships declined and some steam ships were converted to motor propulsion. But a unique survivor means that the process is not complete: SS *Sir Walter Scott* continues to ply on Loch Katrine, as she has done since 1900. She is described in chapter eight. In industry, too, the steam engine has given way to the electric motor. Yet steam power is far from dead: most of the electricity used in Scotland today is generated in steam turbine power stations.

*STEAM PRESERVATION*

*T*he rapid decline of steam power in transport and industry led, perhaps inevitably, to rapid growth of a movement to preserve examples of it before it was too late. Nevertheless, the survival of steam trains, ships and engines in Scotland as things

Preservation milestone: on 4 September 1971 Caledonian Railway 0-4-4 tank locomotive no. 419 was steamed in public for the first time since withdrawal by BR. Conversely, diesel locomotives of the type seen alongside are now history. The location is the Scottish Railway Preservation Society's Falkirk depot.

SCOTTISH RAILWAY PRESERVATION SOCIETY

of the present rather than the past is the result of several interwoven strands.

For a start, steam exhibits have been accumulating in the general collections of national and municipal museums since the last century, when they were first displayed as examples of modern engineering practice. Some of the models then made are themselves now of great historic interest. But the bulk of the movement is modern, established for the most part since the Second World War. The Talyllyn Railway Preservation Society and the Cutty Sark Preservation Society, both formed in the early 1950s, were pioneers among voluntary preservation societies concerned with transport. Their examples were much emulated in Scotland in due course by the Scottish Railway Preservation Society, the Scottish Branch of the Paddle Steamer Preservation Society, and later preservation groups. The common interests of such societies – such as publicity, advice for newcomers, and dealing with officialdom – are promoted by the Association of Railway Preservation Societies Ltd. Generally such preservation groups have a two-part structure, a society to recruit members from the public (often in the form of a company limited by guarantee) and an associated company (often limited by shares) with operating responsibilities – but each is different and generalisation likely to lead to misconceptions.

The steam preservation movement has also been one of individual effort. Several locomotives in Scotland survived because they were purchased on withdrawal by Ian Fraser who eventually found good homes for them. John B. Cameron bought A4 4-6-2 no. 60009, and so ensured that an example of one of the most famous classes of steam locomotive to have worked in Scotland would continue to be seen in action. Nevertheless, the role of British Rail in continued operation of preserved steam locomotives has been equivocal, ranging from a ban during the years immediately following withdrawal of its own locomotives, to relaxation in favour of steam excursions over selected routes and eventual establishment of a scheduled steam train service on the Mallaig line, with today a range of other routes for steam excursions more restricted than formerly.

The role of the individual has probably been greatest in connection with traction engines, though here we are getting into the area of private preservation where, even more than with main line steam excursions, the object of preservation appears in public only intermittently. After the Second World War, traction engines were being bought for what eventually became preservation, though the distinction between operation and preservation was sometimes blurred. When for example the Barrack family haulage business in Aberdeenshire (now JGB Transport) purchased a 1914 Fowler traction engine in 1945, it was the intention to use it for timber extraction. In fact it was used largely for towing, under contract, other redundant traction engines to the scrapyard, but

Traction engine preservation has largely been the province of individuals. This is the driver's view of Bill Barrack's 1914 Fowler.                                                                                           AUTHOR

itself survived to become a favourite in Bill Barrack's collection which in 1988 extended to nine engines.

The Scottish Traction Engine Club was formed in 1961 for people interested in traction engines – it has today about 160 members, of whom perhaps a dozen actually own engines. Four or five traction engine rallies or similar events are organised each year. In practice, membership is concentrated in the central belt. Aberdeenshire traction engine enthusiasts are catered for by the Bon-Accord Steam Engine Club, founded in 1971. At the time of writing, however, the long-term future of this club is uncertain. Its principal activity was organisation of a large traction engine rally annually in Hazlehead Park, Aberdeen, which has been known to attract 25,000 people over two days. It was over-successful: after taking place in particularly bad weather some three years ago, excessive damage to ground and grass made repetition of the event unwelcome. It had been viable because the site attracted enough trade stands to pay the expenses of bringing engines from as far away as Yorkshire: and it has not been possible to find an alternative location close enough to Aberdeen to attract sufficient trade support and visitors. In 1989, however, I understand the club is to host a rally at the Grampian Transport Museum. So road steam appears to be in the doldrums in Scotland so far as large events devoted principally to traction engines are concerned, but participation in special events at other venues of industrial significance which have become established in the past few years, such as Summerlee Heritage Park and the Scottish Mining Museum, appears to be successful, and this is probably the way ahead.

Individuals have also been prominent in the revival of interest which has occurred since the late 1960s in small steam boats and launches. This resulted in 1971 in formation of the Steam Boat Association of Great Britain. Since 1987 members in Scotland have been catered for by its Scottish Branch, under the secretaryship of Harry Watson who runs passenger cruises on Loch Awe with the steam launch *Lady Rowena*. Largely at his instigation, the summers of 1987 and 1988 saw get-togethers of privately-owned steam boats on that loch, and the event seems set to become an annual one. In the case of *Lady Rowena*, individual enthusiasm to operate a steam boat led to establishment of a public service, and much the same happened with the privately-owned Clyde Puffer *VIC 32*, which takes holidaymakers on week-long cruises. So far as I am aware, no-one in the traction engine movement has as yet built a new full-size engine (although many miniature ones have been built, some of them of substantial proportions), but many small steam boats are of new construction, often on traditional lines.

An extreme example of this is perhaps the construction of replicas of three famous pioneer steam boats – two of William Symington's boats, and Henry Bell's *Comet*. The latter was built as long ago as 1962 to celebrate the 150th anniversary of the original. These are also a specialised instance of growing awareness of the importance of the Scottish heritage. Recent years have seen establishment of an increasing number of museums and trusts (which are usually, in legal terms, guarantee companies) dedicated to preservation of the Scottish heritage in one form or another – industrial, maritime, social history, or as it may be. In the activities of many of these, steam power plays an important part against a wider background.

There has been valuable support both for these and for established steam preservation groups from the Manpower Services Commission and its successors. Such support was instrumental in establishment of Summerlee Heritage Park, Coatbridge, and other projects which have benefited (in provision of both men and money) include the Bo'ness & Kinneil Railway, the Scottish Mining Museum, the renovation of the Clyde Puffer *Auld Reekie*, and construction of the replicas of Symington's Dalswinton boat and the *Charlotte Dundas*.

Allied to this an increasing awareness also of the value of steam attractions to tourism. The Scottish Tourist Board has supported, with finance or publicity or both, the Bo'ness & Kinneil Railway, the Paddle Steamer *Waverley*, Auchterarder Heritage Centre Trust (Glenruthven

The Highlands & Islands Development Board is one of several official bodies which have given financial assistance towards the continued operation of steam power. Here HIDB chairman Robert Cowan (extreme right) discusses construction of the Mull railway on site with director Graham Ellis.

MULL & WEST HIGHLAND N.G. RAILWAY

Weaving Mill), the Alford Valley Railway and Kerr's Miniature Railway, Arbroath. The Highlands & Islands Development Board has done likewise in its area for the Strathspey Railway, the Mull railway, *Lady Rowena* and *VIC 32*. These lists are probably not exhaustive. Lest anyone is starting to get the impression that those involved in steam preservation do no more than sit back and wait for the cash handouts to arrive, it is worth noting that several steam groups, quite apart from their individual efforts, got together in 1984 to found the Scotland for Steam group, with a view to joint promotion and marketing. In 1988 nine groups participated, and more have since joined. A combined leaflet is produced every year, and a poster every other year, with the help of British Rail and the Scottish Tourist Board.

Steam preservation in Scotland has been a success story, but only because of continuing undiluted effort by those involved, and there have been casualties along the way. The troubles of the Bon-Accord Steam Engine Club have already been mentioned. After the Waverley Route railway from Edinburgh to Carlisle via Hawick closed in 1969 there was a worthy but almost inevitably unsuccessful attempt to preserve or perpetuate it. A locomotive rested on track left behind by the Admiralty on the island of Hoy, Orkney, for a long time, waiting for a railway which never materialised: it was moved, eventually, to Brechin. A fifteen-inch gauge railway built near Banff closed after a few seasons from lack of passengers. The steamship *Gitana* was raised from the depths of Loch Rannoch, only to sink again – though her steam plant remains ashore.

Over-optimism, clearly, was the fault in many of these schemes, yet it is no more than a virtue carried to excess, and those getting involved with preserving steam power in one form or another certainly need optimism!

It is instructive to look at the passenger or visitor figures for some successful operations, but it is not, on the other hand, easy to do so in a form which compares one with another, because transport undertakings usually count passenger-journeys, that is to say a passenger booking a return ticket makes two passenger-journeys; while those steam attractions offering an out-and-back or circular trip naturally consider the number of bookings the same as the number of passengers. To take first those who count passenger-journeys:

Strathspey Railway: 42,000 in 1987; peak in early '80s of 50,000; 1988 figure, 51,265.

PS *Waverley*: 101,784 in 1987, but season curtailed because of boiler trouble. 157,044 in 1988. Highest figure, 240,000 in 1983. These figures include passengers carried while operating away from Scotland.

Mull & West Highland Railway: over 46,000 in 1988, a substantial increase on 1987.

As a very rough guide, one may assume 60 per cent of the above figures would be approximately comparable with the passenger figures which follow (Strathspey Railway passenger bookings in 1988 were 28,964):

Bo'ness and Kinneil Railway: about 18,000 passengers a year.

SS *Sir Walter Scott*: 48,123 in 1988; 1987 figure was 35,222 and there has been an annual increase since 29,481 in 1983. These figures include one-way passengers as well as those making a round trip or return journey, but the total number of one-way passengers is insignificant.

Kerr's Miniature Railway: about 20,000 passengers a season.

*Lady Rowena*: 3,000 in 1987, probably more in 1988.

SS *VIC 32* carries 250 to 300 people each season on week- or fortnight-long cruises.

The Grampian Transport Museum, Alford, had 25,000 visitors to its main exhibition hall in 1988, but outdoor special events raised the total number of visitors to the site to about 39,000. Glenruthven Weaving Mill (Auchterarder Heritage Centre Trust) gets about 8,000 visitors a year.

The Museum of Transport, Glasgow, re-opened at its new location in the Kelvin Hall in 1988 and (aided, perhaps, by free entry) had no less than 500,000 visitors in its first five months.

In the chapters that follow, a close look is taken at some forty organisations devoted to continued operation of steam power, or the display of relics of steam, in one form or another.

# $M$ U S E U M
# $S$ T E A M

## R O Y A L   M U S E U M   O F   S C O T L A N D

$T$he Royal Museum of Scotland, Chambers Street, Edinburgh, dates from as long ago as 1854, when it was set up as the Industrial Museum of Scotland. This was intended to be a museum of contemporary technology, of educational importance: it had close links with Edinburgh University (the first director was also a university professor) and to this day there is a physical link with the adjoining university building in the form of a bridge over the intervening street, although this is now blanked off on the university side. The museum subsequently became the Museum of Science & Art, and then the Royal Scottish Museum. In 1986 it merged with the National Museum of Antiquities of Scotland (Queen Street, Edinburgh) to become the Royal Museum of Scotland. This is the principal component of the National Museums of Scotland, administered by trustees but funded by the Scottish Education Department, and with free admission.

Over the years the Chambers Street museum has assembled, among its many other exhibits, a good representative collection to illustrate the development of steam engines and their application to industrial, railway, marine and road use. It comprises both full-size exhibits and models. The collection is divided between the Hall of Power which, as you enter the building by its Main Hall, is away down to the right, and Victorian Engineering which is straight ahead. It is not, unfortunately, laid out in any clear order to enable development to be followed easily, nor is any large-scale re-arrangement likely as the museum has commitments in other directions, and in any case Victorian Engineering is to be closed for about a year for roof repairs; some of the exhibits will be displayed temporarily elsewhere in the museum. In this book it is not of course possible to list all the steam exhibits, either at this museum or at other locations described subsequently, but mention of the most important is essential.

The best way to start a visit to the Chambers Street museum is to enter the Hall of Power and bear round to the right. Here is a display case of models and display placards relating to the earliest steam pumps, starting with Savery's pre-Newcomen pump which was intended to drain mines. Steam was to be condensed in a chamber, so that atmospheric pressure would force water up a pipe into it past a non-return valve; more steam was then to be admitted to force the water still higher. Contemporary technology was inadequate to make it work, but there is also on display a full-size sectioned Pulsometer, a nineteenth-century revival of the principle made practicable by improved engineering techniques. The same case contains material relating to early beam engines, and to Trevithick's pioneering high pressure engines built around 1800. Nearby are full-size stationary steam engines dating from the first half of the nineteenth century. Notable among them is a small beam engine of the 1840s typical of factory power of that period: it worked at St Leo-

By the 1840s small beam engines such as this were providing power in factories. This one was installed second-hand in St Leonards Brewery, Edinburgh, in 1867 and worked until 1933; it is now in the Royal Museum of Scotland.

Early Parsons steam turbine coupled to dynamo was originally used to provide electric light on a warship launched in 1890; it is now in the Royal Museum of Scotland.

nard's Brewery, Edinburgh, from 1867 until 1933 when it was presented to the museum. The Victorian Engineering hall also contains several stationary engines of various types, and a delightful small portable engine which was made, probably in the late 1880s, by Tuxford of Boston, Lincs. Nothing is known of its history prior to presentation to the museum in 1951, but it is likely that it worked on a Scottish farm. Nearby is a Parsons steam turbine, coupled directly to a dynamo: it was used originally to generate electricity for lighting on HMS *Gossamer* which was launched in 1890. Applications of this type were the first for which the steam turbine was used: in this example part of the casing has been cut away to reveal the blades, against which steam impinges to make the rotor rotate.

Of railway material, by far the most remarkable is the locomotive *Wylam Dilly* in the Hall of Power. This and the similar locomotive *Puffing Billy* in the Science Museum, London, are the two oldest surviving locomotives. Which of the two is older has long since been forgotten, but both were built about 1814 by William Hedley for the coal-carrying Wylam Waggonway near Newcastle upon Tyne. Vertical cylinders and drive through overhead beams reflect stationary engine practice of the period. The locomotive was purchased by Hedley's sons after she ceased work in the late 1860s, and came to the museum in 1882.

Subsequent locomotive development is displayed in the form of models, of which two are particularly interesting. The locomotive *Edina* in Victorian Engineering is a contemporary and very fine model of a typical Stephenson-type locomotive of the 1840s. Nearby is North British Railway 4-4-0 *Abbotsford*, built in the museum workshops in 1883 to drawings supplied by the railway company and signed by Locomotive Superintendent Dugald Drummond. These are still held by the museum. Drummond had designed and built the first of the class in 1876, to haul express trains over the Waverley Route from Edinburgh to Carlisle, the 98 miles of which they covered non-stop in 2 hours 20 minutes. (By 1962, the best time for this run was 2 hours 53 minutes, admittedly with several stops, but nevertheless backward progress which may well have made its own peculiar contribution to closure of the line a few years later.) The boiler of the model is sectioned to enable its construction to be studied – no doubt what the museum originally required was an instructional model. It is still valuable for that purpose, in the absence of any full size sectioned steam locomotive in Scotland. Those who wish to study the operation of steam engine valves and valve gears may do so from instructional models in the Hall of Power.

Marine steam is represented by among others a very fine model of an 1870s three-cylinder compound engine in the Hall of Power, and a model in Victorian Engineering of a triple expansion engine of 1900 for a destroyer, described as the peak of steam engine design. Nearby the destroyer HMS *Handy* of 1895 appears in the form of a builder's model. (The significance of such models is mentioned on page 30.) In this hall too is a partly-sectioned model of the steam dredger *Manchester* of 1890.

Steam road vehicles commence in the Hall of Power with a model of Cugnot's premature vehicle of 1770, which ran in Paris and was intended to carry artillery. There is also a replica of William Murdock's working model steam vehicle of c. 1784. The original survives in Birmingham Science Museum. Murdock, a Scot, was Boulton & Watt's best erector of steam engines, but was successfully leant on by his employers to desist from developing a full-size steam carriage.

There are several most interesting exhibits in the Hall of Power from the era of steam cars. These include Serpollet and White steam car engines and, particularly, a complete Locomobile steam car built in the USA about 1900. The two-cylinder vertical engine is positioned beneath the seat, and the rear wheels are driven by chain through a differential. The tubular steel of the chassis is derived from contemporary bicycle manufacturing practice, but the layout of the chassis, rigid and unsprung, with the body mounted on springs above it, is no advance on horse-drawn coaches of a century earlier. Petrol fuel was used in the

The Royal Museum of Scotland's Locomobile steam car was built in the USA about 1900. Panelling has been removed to reveal the two-cylinder engine beneath the seat; condenser occupies the position of the radiator on an i/c engined vehicle.

simple firetube boiler. This type of car was designed and at first built by the brothers F.E. and F.O. Stanley, who sold manufacturing rights to Locomobile about 1899 and bought them back again in 1902. The museum's example bears the inscription 'Supplied by Lawrence Bell, Gas & Motor engineer, Innerleithen'; museum records state that it was presented to the museum in 1925 by Mr Lawrence Bell of Edinburgh, who seems likely to have been the same person. Perhaps it was a demonstration model.

In addition to those on display, the National Museums have several stationary steam engines in store, and a Marshall single cylinder agricultural traction engine of 1907 which spent most of its working life in Scotland. It is intended to restore the latter to working order and display it at the Scottish Agricultural Museum (part of the National Museums) which already holds threshing tackle of the type once powered, and towed from farm to farm, by traction engines. Biggar Gasworks Museum is part of the National Museums and has some working steam engines. It is mentioned in a later chapter, as are the Bo'ness & Kinneil railway where are to be found two steam locomotives and the former boiler of the paddle steamer *Waverley,* belonging to the National Museums, and Summerlee Heritage Park which has a National Museums steam crane on loan.

$I$n the Scottish governmental machine, operation of museums other than the National Museums is the responsibility of district councils. Their powers are permissive rather than mandatory, and one of the consequences is that City of Glasgow District Council spends more on museums than all the other district councils put together – or so we are informed by *Museums in Scotland,* a report by the Museums and Galleries Commission. In the absence of any national comprehensive transport museum, Glasgow's Museum of Transport goes a long way towards filling the gap – although it is arguable that the history of transport in and around Glasgow reflects that of Scotland as a whole, not only in the vehicles and vessels operated but also in their construction.

Establishment of the Museum of Transport was prompted by closure of the city's electric tramway system in 1962 and a desire to preserve some of its trams. The museum was opened in 1964 by the then Corporation of the City of Glasgow in the former tramway works in Albert Drive. But Glasgow had been accumulating historical engineering material since 1870: the collection had been housed since 1902 in its Kelvingrove Art Gallery & Museum. Transport items from this were gradually passed to the Transport Museum, which was also presented with five full-size locomotives by British Rail. The new museum's collection, which covers most forms of transport, continued to expand and by the mid-1980s the museum had outgrown the Albert Drive building, which was deteriorating; while the Kelvin Hall, formerly used for trade exhibitions and the like, was vacant following completion of the Scottish Exhibition Centre. Part of the Kelvin Hall was then reconditioned for the Museum of Transport (the remainder has become a sports and recreation complex) and certain large exhibits in the Glasgow engineering collection were placed on loan with Summerlee Heritage Trust and the Scottish Maritime Museum, under which headings they are mentioned. The Museum of Transport re-opened at the Kelvin Hall in April 1988; ceremonial re-opening by HRH the Duchess of Gloucester followed in September.

Highland Railway 'Jones Goods' no. 103 was both the first 4-6-0 built for use in Britain, and the most powerful locomotive on a British railway, when completed in 1894. She is now preserved in the Museum of Transport, Glasgow.

MUSEUM OF TRANSPORT, GLASGOW

So far as steam exhibits are concerned, it is of course the locomotives that are most prominent. Back in the mid-1950s British Railways, although embarking on a comprehensive modernisation plan, found time to restore some historic locomotives to running order, principally to haul specials. Scottish Region in particular restored two pre-grouping locomotives which had been preserved since withdrawal by the LMS in the 1930s – Caledonian Railway 4-2-2 no. 123, and Highland Railway 'Jones Goods' 4-6-0 no. 103 – and repainted two more pre-grouping locomotives, until then still in normal service, in the liveries of their former owners: Great North of Scotland Railway 4-4-0 no. 49 *Gordon Highlander* and North British Railway 4-4-0 no. 256 *Glen Douglas*. They were then used to haul special trains (and occasionally ordinary ones) until steam locomotives were withdrawn from general service in Scotland.

These locomotives represented four of the five main pre-grouping railway companies in Scotland. By the mid-1960s no locomotives from the fifth, the Glasgow & South Western, survived in BR service but one was located which had been sold by the LMS in 1934 because it was one of a small class, non-standard and therefore expensive to maintain. This locomotive, 0-6-0 tank locomotive no. 9, had run for many years at a Welsh colliery and was lying out of use. At the instigation of the late John Scholes, curator of the then Museum of British Transport at Clapham, London, it was recovered for preservation and all five locomotives were moved to the Glasgow Museum of Transport. They went on public display there in 1967.

Three out of these five locomotives formerly belonged to railways which served Glasgow, and all of them were built there. In two of them, the museum has locomotives of specific historic interest. Fast lightweight CR no. 123 was built for the 1886 Edinburgh International Exhibition, used on expresses between Edinburgh and Carlisle via Beattock, and later on directors' specials and as royal train pilot, running ahead of the royal train to ensure that the way was clear. Highland Railway 103 was probably the most powerful main line locomotive in Britain when built in1894: it was the first of a class of locomotives introduced by HR locomotive superintendent David Jones for the arduous Perth-Inverness line, principally for goods trains although they were also used on passenger trains. They were the first locomotives in Britain of the 4-6-0 wheel arrangement, which was much used subsequently. It is not clear why it was repainted in the Highland Railway's yellow livery, which Jones had replaced by green some nine years before 103 was built. The two 4-4-0s, which were built in 1913 (*Glen Douglas*) and 1920 (*Gordon Highlander*), are by contrast almost equally valuable as examples of typical passenger locomotives of their period.

These five locomotives have been joined in the Museum of Transport by others: a light vertical-boilered locomotive, built in Glasgow, which spent most of its life shunting wagons at Northampton gas works, and a fireless locomotive, intended for shunting in places where there was a fire risk, and at the same time a supply of steam available to recharge at intervals the steam reservoir which replaces the boiler. This particular example was built for a munitions factory.

A further locomotive, Caledonian Railway 0-6-0 no. 828, was purchased from British Rail during the 1960s by the Scottish Locomotive Preservation Trust Fund and loaned to the museum. However it was eventually transferred to the Strathspey Railway, where it is being restored to working order. Principal difficulties in the way of restoring the museum's own locomotives to steam appear to be the expense of removal, and eventual re-installation, in a museum which is not rail-connected, and the length of time during which, for such an exercise to be worthwhile, one or more locomotives would have to be missing from a collection best appreciated as a group.

There is, in the author's opinion, another consideration. There are now several locations in Scotland where it is possible to see locomotives in steam and travel in steam-hauled trains. Restoring a locomotive to steam means replacing worn parts by new ones, and running it means that parts from bearings to boiler immediately start to deteriorate, and have steadily to be replaced. So long as some locomotives are running, it seems to me that there is a good case for not running others, for leaving them as received from BR and maintaining their historic integrity as long as possible, in museum conditions. Certainly in this way the Glasgow museum locomotives are seen by a great many more visitors than would be likely if they were elsewhere. On the other hand, movement is such a vital part of the transport scene that it does seem that a transport museum where everything appears to be static lacks an important element. It is good news that it is intended to use the museum's lecture theatre (which is entered, delightfully, through the Regal Cinema entrance which forms part of a 1938-period street) to show video recordings made from films of historic transport in action – including film of the museum's locomotives when operating on BR around 1960. It is intended also to construct a working model railway.

Among its other railway exhibits, the museum contains the royal saloon formerly used by the Duke of Edinburgh, and an excellent collection of railway permanent way materials.

Although the locomotives are the most prominent, the most important exhibit in terms of the history of steam transport is one of the least conspicuous. This is the chassis of a steam 'drag', or towing vehicle for passenger coaches, built for road use by Goldsworthy Gurney about 1830. It is I believe unique, the only large relic to survive from the early period of steam coach development, which lasted from the late eighteenth century until the 1840s. Gurney was one of the great protagonists of steam coaches, and in the 1820s developed the layout exemplified in this chassis, two horizontal cylinders between the frames driving onto a crank axle, at a period when locomotive engineers were still stuck with cylinders which were vertical or inclined, *Rocket*-style, at 45 degrees. Engineers such as Robert Stephenson were much influenced by Gurney's work and adopted his layout for locomotives. This particular steam drag was brought to Scotland in 1831 with the intention of starting a steam road coach service between Edinburgh and Glasgow. It had, however, been damaged during the sea voyage north, and was tampered with by unauthorised persons with the result that the boiler exploded. The chassis was eventually presented to Glasgow Museums in 1889.

The steam drag chassis accompanies four twentieth-century steam road vehicles: a 1920 Ruston & Hornsby traction engine, a 1931 Aveling

Frames and horizontal engine of Gurney steam drag of c.1830 preserved at the Museum of Transport, Glasgow, are a unique relic of the steam road vehicles developed at that period. Early locomotive designers such as Robert Stephenson adopted the layout from them.                                    AUTHOR

& Porter steam roller, a Sentinel steam wagon and a Stanley steam car of c. 1919. Externally a typical car of its period, it makes an interesting comparison with the earlier Stanley-designed Locomobile in the Royal Museum of Scotland; at the time of its construction, the Stanley company was producing steam cars at a rate of 600 a year. The fire appliance section of the museum includes two steam-powered horse-drawn fire fighting pumps.

Having got this far, the visitor to the museum might be pardoned for supposing he was reaching the end of the line: in fact, one of the most interesting and historically valuable parts of the museum still awaits him. This, entered on the first floor, is the Clyde Room with its collection of ship models. Not just ordinary models, but for the most part builders' models. It was the practice of shipbuilders to maintain model-making departments which made models of projected or new ships, to demonstrate to potential purchasers how a proposed vessel would appear, or to adorn the sales offices of shipping lines. Such models ranged from plain half-block models to models which were very finely detailed indeed, and if they had been made by Clyde shipbuilders they tended eventually to find their way to Glasgow Corporation's museum, so that today the collection totals some 685 models, most of them builders' models, and a selection of about 150 of the most important is on display.

It is very easy to pass too quickly through the Clyde Room, when in truth there is scarcely a model there which does not repay close examination. The collection includes ships of all types, and of those that were not actually built on the Clyde most would have traded there during their working lives. So one can study here the development of the steamship in outline from *Comet* to *QE II*, taking in on the way passenger liners, cargo ships, warships, yachts and specialised vessels such as dredgers. And nearly all the models bear the stamp of authenticity, of having been built by the shipbuilders themselves at the same period as the originals.

There is one group, however, which is in the present context particularly interesting – the Clyde river steamers. For nearly 150 years the Clyde steamers not only provided an essential transport service to the coastal towns and islands of the firth, but were public favourites as the means of access to its holiday resorts (to the development of which they contributed greatly), and for pleasure cruising. Towards the end of the last century, most services came under control of one or other of the railway companies, and were operated in connection with their trains. Of all the Clyde steamers, however, the only full size survivor in working order is PS *Waverley*. But in the Clyde Room one encounters famous Clyde steamers from the past – *Columba, Iona,* and *King Edward* the first commercial turbine steamship, built in 1901, among others. The favourite, perhaps, is the 1:32 scale (larger than most) model of PS *Glen Sannox*, displayed in the striking pale grey livery of the Glasgow & South Western Railway for which the original was built in 1891. In her day she was the fastest ship on the Clyde.

*T*he McLean is now the responsibility of Inverclyde District Council, but it is old-established and has been accumulating its collections for over a century. It contains a remarkably fine fine-art collection, but it also has a collection of steam engines, full-size and model, associated with the local shipbuilding and related industries, from which many of its benefactors derived their wealth.

The art collection contains two striking paintings of interest here for their spirited portrayal of steamships of the late 1840s. In 1847 Queen Victoria visited the Clyde, and the scene is recorded in *Queen's Visit to the Clyde* by William Clark and *The Royal Squadron passing Gourock* by Robert Knox, the former including at least ten steamships and the latter seven. Both artists made the most of the accompanying smoke and steam and the paintings provide an all too rare opportunity to see how steamships of that period appeared in action.

Among the steam engines, two full-size engines, one with a single vertical cylinder and 'A' frames, the other with twin inverted oscillating cylinders, were formerly used to operate pumps at a local dry dock. There is also a small compound engine of the type used to power steam launches, built by H. Guy of Cowes IoW. A working model of a compound beam engine dates from as early as 1838, and later models exemplify the development of the marine engine. They are complemented by several fine ship models, including one of PS *Mona's Isle*, the original of which was built in 1882 by Greenock shipbuilders Caird & Co. Members of the Caird family were among the McLean's greatest benefactors.

The museum has some relics of James Watt, whose birthplace was Greenock: notably his chemical balance, and a brace and a set of bits, drill stocks and drills which he gave to an engineer friend, Robert Hart, and his brother as a mark of regard. It also has relics of another pioneer who worked in the vicinity, Henry Bell, in the form of a portrait and an early model of the *Comet*. The McLean Museum & Art Gallery was closed for renovation during 1988, but is expected to re-open during 1989.

*S*pringburn Museum is a good local community museum, in a community where much has changed. For Springburn was formerly the locomotive-building centre of Glasgow – many would say of Britain. There the Edinburgh & Glasgow Railway established its Cowlairs Works in the early 1840s, and at Cowlairs shortly before it closed in 1966 British Rail for the last time repaired steam locomotives in Scotland. Meanwhile the Caledonian Railway had established its St Rollox Works in Springburn in 1853, to become eventually British Rail's Glasgow Works; and when in 1903 three independent locomotive builders in Springburn merged to form the North British Locomotive Company there was no larger locomotive building firm outside the USA. North British built 570 locomotives in 1905, but in the depression year of 1933 was down to a mere sixteen – remarkable even in an industry notorious for its cyclical nature. The company survived to enjoy a brief boom after the Second World War, but failed to make the change from steam power to diesel and went into liquidation in 1962. Today its former head office building in Flemington Street survives, complete with a facade incorporating a head-on view of a steam locomotive in stone, as the regional council's Springburn College.

Springburn Museum shares a building with Springburn Library not far away in Atlas Square, Ayr Street. It was opened in 1986 and is operated by the Springburn Museum Trust, with financial support from Glasgow District Council and the Scottish Office. The museum's displays of photographs, artefacts and models tell the story not only of the locomotive building industry itself, but also of the social history of the community which grew up around it and depended upon it. Exhibits change every two months or so.

The museum's project for 1990 is the repatriation of an exported North British Loco. Co. steam locomotive: specifically, a 4-8-2 built in 1930 for the 3 ft 6 in. gauge Rhodesia Railways and at the time of writing lying out of use in Zambia. It is hoped that this would be exhibited at Atlas Square, on the site of NBL's Hyde Park works, and so would become the only locomotive, built in Scotland for export, to return to the country in which it was built. It is hoped, too, to return it eventually to working order.

The museum also publishes a series of information sheets, one of which (No. 3 *Cowlairs Works*) gives an extremely good description of the process of manufacturing steam locomotives – from technical drawings and pattern shop to erecting shop, weighing shop and testing out on the line.

# *B O ' N E S S   T H E*
# *&   S C O T T I S H*
# *K I N N E I L :   R A I L W A Y*
# *P R E S E R V A T I O N*
# *S O C I E T Y*

*T H E   P I O N E E R S*

*T*he Scottish Railway Preservation Society is the oldest-established voluntary group of its kind in Scotland: in consequence, it has the most extensive, most interesting and most representative collection of locomotives, rolling stock, buildings and other railway artefacts. By 1988 this included twenty three steam locomotives. For many years SRPS locomotives and coaches have run on railtours over British Rail, sometimes separately, sometimes together; and after a long search, the society has established its own branch line, the Bo'ness & Kinneil Railway, over which to operate a regular train service which not merely carries passengers but demonstrates historic locomotives and coaches in action. But although this is operational and much has been achieved, it is still far from complete and the society deserves all the support it can get.

The SRPS was founded in November 1961 to save, restore and eventually to operate items representative of the Scottish railway scene. In 1974 it became a charity and was incorporated as a company limited by guarantee, the word 'Limited' being omitted from its title by licence of the Department of Trade. At this point its main objects were stated more formally: 'To preserve and restore, to original condition wherever possible, locomotives, rolling stock and other equipment and relics of railways in Scotland, as may illustrate the characteristics of her railways and the course of her railway history, or which are of actual or potential historic, scientific or educational value or importance.' Further objects include displaying such items to the public and demonstrating their working, carrying the public, establishing and maintaining 'for the benefit of the nation' a static or operating museum, and constructing, maintaining and working railway lines, buildings and other structures.

Support increased gradually at first, but by 1964 the society was able to open a small relics museum in the closed Murrayfield station in Edinburgh. This proved a false start, for attempted break-ins, and fears of vandalism to a wooden building, were to lead to closure of the museum five years later. In the meantime, however, the society had obtained the building which was to become its base – and indeed almost synonymous with the SRPS – for more than twenty years. This was the former goods transhipment shed at Wallace Street, Falkirk: rail-connected and intended at first to be the large relics museum, limited security of tenure meant that it became rather the depot in which the society's growing collection of locomotives and rolling stock was stored, restored and maintained, with open days for the public at intervals.

At that stage the society had decided to concentrate on building up a collection of locomotives and rolling stock. In this of course it was quite right, for at the time, astonishing though it seems in retrospect, locomotives and rolling stock which had originated with the pre-grouping companies were still in service and familiar, though it was clear that they would not survive for long.

The first locomotive to arrive at the Falkirk depot was 419, in the Caledonian Railway's numeration. More recently she had been, grimy and run-down, British Railways no. 55189, withdrawn from service at Carstairs late in December 1962. But she was of Caledonian Railway origin, built in 1907, one of what had been a large class of 0-4-4 tank locomotives used throughout its system on local passenger trains. In November 1962 the SRPS launched a fund to purchase her on with-drawal. By the spring of 1964 it had raised only £100 towards the asking price of £600, but the locomotive was still in store. The society's honor-ary president the late Mr W.E.C. Watkinson, a Worcestershire farmer with a love of Scotland and Scottish Railways, stepped in with a loan (eventually converted into a gift) of £500 to complete the purchase. Watkinson did more: he donated a further £750 for the locomotive to be restored in British Railways workshops. Even in those days that was not enough for a full overhaul to running order, but some mechanical work was done, and then the locomotive went into the paintshop. What emerged was a chrysalis to butterfly transformation – except that in this case 419 had been restored to her original appearance, gorgeous in the Caledonian Railway Company's deep Prussian Blue, set off by black and white lining-out and red-brown buffer beams. She was delivered to Falkirk in April 1965. Seeing her, people began to realise that the SRPS was serious.

North British Railway 0-6-0 *Maude* and train stand at Birkhill station, Bo'ness &
Kinneil Railway, while filming for television in September 1988 before the station
was opened.                                                                        AUTHOR

No. 419 was joined at Falkirk in 1967 by former North British Railway
0-6-0 goods locomotive *Maude*. This locomotive had been built earlier
than 419 – as the NBR's no. 673 in 1891 – and survived slightly longer,
as British Railways no. 65243, until 1966. The name was given her after
service abroad during the First World War, being the surname of the
famous general. A few others of the class received comparable names –
but only a few, for the J36 class was large and long-lived. Reference to
Ian Allan's *ABC* for 1952 shows 100 of these locomotives still then at
work. *Maude*, the sole survivor, is typical of late Victorian Scottish goods
locomotives, of the locomotives in other words which performed the
essential task of moving the country's freight in perhaps the most
prosperous period it has seen.

*Maude* and 419 were the first of what was to become a growing collection of locomotives, many of them of industrial railway origin. The 0-4-0
tank locomotive *Ellesmere* had been built by Hawthorn's of Leith as early

as 1861, and was the oldest Scottish-built locomotive to survive. She had spent her working life in Lancashire until withdrawn in 1957. The 0-4-0 saddle tank locomotive no. 13, on the other hand, presented to the society by the National Coal Board in 1968 was the first locomotive to reach the SRPS in running order. She was steamed by society members on several occasions, until one of the crankpins broke. Repairs were decided upon: David Stirling, writing in the society's magazine *Blastpipe* in 1988, recalled that in the absence of an electricity supply it took three months of weekend work with a ratchet drill to drill out the crankpin. By the time a second crankpin had to be dealt with, members had purchased a diesel generator: the same task took about three days. In 1971 work started on restoring 419 to steam. She eventually reappeared in steam, in public, for the first time in September 1972. Gradually, the society was accumulating the tools and the skills to maintain its collection.

Thus the SRPS collection of locomotives was built up. One of the most notable arrivals subsequently was D49 class 4-4-0 no. 246 *Morayshire* which had been built by the LNER at Darlington in 1928. Much of her working life was spent in Scotland, and when she was withdrawn in 1961 she was the last survivor of the class. She was saved from the scrapheap when she was bought by Ian Fraser of Arbroath, who had served his apprenticeship at Darlington and worked on that class of locomotive. In 1966 he presented her to the then Royal Scottish Museum, which however could only place her in store. By the mid-1970s SRPS techniques and abilities in locomotive maintenance were well enough established for the national museum to be willing to loan this locomotive to the society so that she might be returned to steam. Her eventual return to main line operation is described in chapter five, as is the contribution of the Scottish Railway Preservation Society to this subject generally, for since 1972 some of its locomotives had been allowed out on to the main line.

In parallel with its collection of locomotives, the society had been building up a collection of coaches and wagons. Once again, it is remarkable that, starting in the 1960s, it was able to acquire passenger coaches which had been operated by all five of the principal pre-grouping Scottish railways. It was also able to obtain several coaches of both LMS and LNER origin. A comparable collection of goods vehicles was also built up, many of them dating from the early years of the present century or the latter part of the last.

*I*n 1967 the SRPS learned that the
Highlands & Islands Development Board wished to support re-opening
the railway from Aviemore to Boat of Garten. This had formed part of the
original Highland Railway main line from Perth to Inverness via Aviemore, Grantown-on-Spey and Forres, completed in 1863, but it had lost
much of its importance with the opening of the direct line from Aviemore to Inverness via Carrbridge in 1898. Aviemore to Forres was eventually closed to passenger traffic in 1965 under the Beeching plan, and
to freight also beyond Boat of Garten. From Aviemore as far as Boat it
remained open to freight for a while to serve distilleries down the Great
North of Scotland Railway Speyside line, which diverged at Boat; but
these sections too were closed to all traffic in 1968.

Meanwhile in 1965 the newly-formed Highlands & Islands Development Board was promoting tourism in Aviemore and district, and
started to look into the possibility of continuing the passenger train service between Aviemore and Grantown-on-Spey. But it did not wish to
buy the line: rather, it sought another organization to which it could
give financial aid for re-opening the line from Aviemore to Grantown
with diesel passenger trains, and it invited the Scottish Railway Preservation Society to run historic steam trains between Aviemore and Boat
of Garten.

As negotiations continued, however, proposals were modified: the
SRPS would form a company, the Strathspey Railway Company, to operate the line from the north end of Aviemore station to Boat of Garten
only; the purchase price of the line was expected to be about £40,000
which did not seem cheap in those days, although the Highland Board
was to contribute a grant of £10,000 and a loan of £20,000. In 1970 the
SRPS decided to proceed, subject to satisfactory negotiations with British Railways and the HIDB. But many members were becoming more
and more uneasy at the gradual shift from running trains on someone
else's railway to taking full responsibility for a railway so far away. In May
1971 in general meeting the society decided to abandon the negotiations.

Four years of negotiations did not prove totally abortive. On the one
hand, some of those who favoured the scheme decided to go it alone:
and the eventual success of the Strathspey Railway is described in chapter six. On the other, the society had learned a lot, and started to look for
a site in central Scotland on a disused railway where a depot could be
established and an operating line set up as effort and funds permitted.

Possibilities considered included the Haddington branch, and Bo'ness Junction (on the main Edinburgh-Glasgow line) to Kinneil – but the line which seemed most attractive was from Alloa to Dollar.

However, funds for the venture proved difficult to raise, and it seems that much of the money that was raised was swallowed up by expenses. Nevertheless the Glenochil Railway Co. Ltd. was incorporated in October 1975, with an authorised capital of £125,000 in £10 shares and its main object 'to purchase or otherwise acquire . . . maintain . . . and work for the conveyance of passengers goods livestock and all kinds of merchandise the railway line between Alloa and Dollar and any other railway line wheresoever situated. . . .' Some (but not a majority) of its directors were to be nominated by the SRPS: in practice, all three original directors were also SRPS directors.

Perhaps the bit about 'any other railway line' was prophetic. At any rate, by 1977 hopes for Alloa-Dollar had been replaced by plans for a railway on the foreshore at Bo'ness (Borrowstounness, in full), and in July 1978 the name of the company was changed to the Bo'ness & Kinneil Railway Co. Ltd. By 1986, however, the company had not traded: what it had done was to raise funds by issue of shares, which funds were then loaned to the SRPS to assist it in developing the railway at Bo'ness.

The origins of railways at Bo'ness are found in the dawn of Scottish railways, before there was any sort of national network, but when a small network of local lines had grown up centred on the coal mines and ironworks of the Monklands. An eastward projection from this, the Slamannan Railway, was opened in 1840 to Causewayend Basin on the Union Canal, and in 1851 extended to Bo'ness. Meanwhile the Edinburgh & Glasgow Railway, the first trunk railway in Scotland, had been opened in 1842, and the Slamannan's extension passed beneath it at Manuel; a connecting curve was put in to the E & G at Bo'ness Junction. Eventually a series of amalgamations took both companies into the North British Railway, and so into the LNER.

For many years the port of Bo'ness was busy exporting coal and importing timber. But passenger trains south of Manuel were withdrawn in 1930, though they continued to run between Bo'ness and Polmont, which is on the Edinburgh & Glasgow main line, until 1956. The same year the harbour was closed, and in 1965 freight services were cut back to terminate at Kinneil colliery, the final mile or so of line to Bo'ness being closed. Coal trains from Kinneil colliery eventually ceased in June 1978 but the line was not formally closed until there seemed no prospect of their resumption, which meant October 1980. During this final period special trains of Scottish Railway Preservation Society rolling stock ran from Falkirk to Kinneil in August 1978, and

An early stage in construction of Bo'ness station by the Scottish Railway Preservation Society, during the winter of 1979-80.                                ANDREW HARPER

again a year later, for the society was already focusing its attention on Bo'ness and its branch line.

However, at Bo'ness itself, the once-extensive railway system had been swept away: what the society was doing was building a new railway on what was not so much a green field site as greenish urban dereliction site, then being landscaped. The land belonged and belongs to the local authorities – most of it to Falkirk District, but with a patch belonging to Central Region – and has been leased to the SRPS. The new railway, just under $1\frac{1}{2}$ miles long, was to start from a new terminus further east than the old passenger station, and, following only approximately the course of the old, run to Kinneil. There it had been hoped originally to make link with British Rail; but closure of the line to Manuel meant that the SRPS was able to negotiate with British Rail for its acquisition also, with eventual success.

Meanwhile planning permission for Bo'ness & Kinneil was obtained in 1978 and work started in May 1979, the first task being to erect the fencing for a security compound. From this start has developed a small town terminus. Nothing at Bo'ness station is original, on that site: much has been brought in from elsewhere. The station building was originally at Wormit: it was dismantled by society members and re-erected at Bo'ness during 1981. The large locomotive shed – used for repairs as well as storage – was built new, but to traditional appearance. The foot-bridge was originally at Murthly, and has additions from Dunbar; the signal box was formerly at Garnqueen South Junction, the water column at Grangemouth. The goods shed – or what appears externally to be the goods shed, for internally it is used as a joiner's shop – is new, built of sandstone from buildings demolished locally.

Historically the most significant building is the train shed spanning platform and tracks, which formed part of Edinburgh's first main line station, the Haymarket terminus of the Edinburgh & Glasgow Railway opened in 1842. The train shed is typical of its period and remained in situ, latterly covering only part of the car park, until 1982. Then, when the station was rebuilt, it was dismantled, and reconstructed at Bo'ness.

Much of the work has been done voluntarily by the society's members. Much has also been done by Manpower Services Commission schemes and the like. As the railway progressed, locomotives and rolling stock were brought from Falkirk, and the station building, platform and track leading from it were sufficiently far advanced for Bo'ness station to be opened to the public, with a shuttle train service, on 27 June 1981. Work continued on extending the line, and the train service, by stages; it was delayed while concrete rafts were built over a pipeline which the railway had to cross, and the track eventually reached the new station at Kinneil in 1985. The line was formally opened by Mr Chris Green, then general manager of ScotRail, on 29 June, and a public service operated over that weekend by special permission of the Railway Inspectorate; a regular public service had to wait until the following Easter, after the Bo'ness & Kinneil Light Railway Order, made in response to an application by Falkirk District Council, Central Regional Council and the SRPS, came into operation in January 1986. (Light railway order procedure, which originated in the 1890s as a means to authorise rural branch lines without the expense of private Acts of Parliament, has been adopted by preserved steam railways; the government's Railway Inspectorate is responsible for inspecting new passenger railways before they are opened.)

By 1986, newly acquired locomotives and rolling stock were being delivered direct to Bo'ness. The most notable arrival was the Scandinavian vintage train. In the 1980s, the supply of British steam locomotives, other than industrials, had virtually dried up: to obtain a locomotive in anything resembling working order it was necessary to look abroad. Fortunately the Bo'ness & Kinneil Railway is one of very few British steam railways with a loading gauge ample enough for foreign locomotives. Fortunately too the Swedish State Railways had in store a strategic reserve of steam locomotives, from which they were willing to sell to SRPS member Willie Crawford B class 4-6-0 no. 1313. She arrived at Bo'ness in 1981, and was subsequently joined by a train of handsome wooden-bodied passenger coaches from Norwegian State Railways.

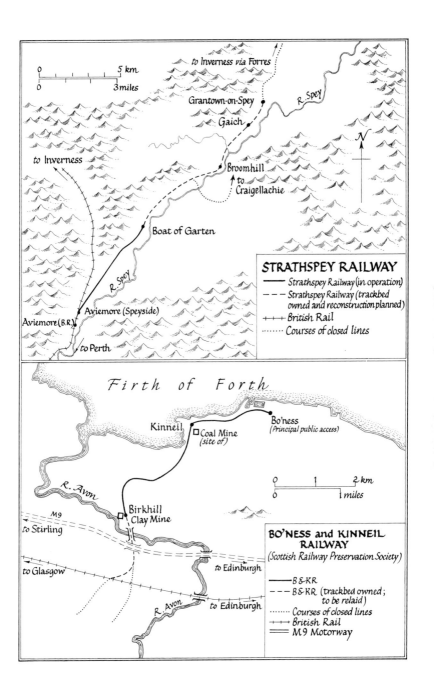

0 5 km
0 3 miles

to Inverness via Forres

Grantown-on-Spey
Gaich
R. Spey

N

to Inverness

Broomhill
to
Craigellachie

Boat of Garten

R. Spey

## STRATHSPEY RAILWAY

— Strathspey Railway (in operation)
- - - Strathspey Railway (trackbed owned and reconstruction planned)
+++ British Rail
······ Courses of closed lines

Aviemore (Speyside)
Aviemore (B.R.)
to Perth

Firth of Forth

Kinneil
Coal Mine
(site of)

Bo'ness
(Principal public access)

R. Avon

M9
to Stirling

Birkhill
Clay Mine

to Glasgow

to Edinburgh

R. Avon

to Edinburgh

## BO'NESS and KINNEIL RAILWAY
(Scottish Railway Preservation Society)

—— B & KR
- - - B & KR (trackbed owned; to be relaid)
······ Courses of closed lines
+++ British Rail
═══ M9 Motorway

Although the locomotive was over-large for the shuttle service along the foreshore (but will no doubt come into her own on the longer and more steeply graded line to Manuel) the coaches have proved well-suited to the line and have seen regular use. The latter is also true of one of the most recent additions to the locomotive stock, 0-6-0 saddle tank locomotive no. 19 presented by the National Coal Board in 1985. She is one of the 'Austerity' locomotives designed for the wartime Ministry of Supply in 1942, powerful, simple easily-maintained locomotives as popular with latter-day users of steam power as they are with present-day preserved railways.

By the time regular trains to Kinneil station started in 1986, the line had been extended to join the old branch line near the site of Kinneil colliery. The track no longer, unfortunately, extended as far as Manuel, for available finance had permitted purchase only of the trackbed of the line together with track in situ for the first one and a half miles from Kinneil and along the viaduct over the River Avon, where suitable check rail chairs, once lost, would have been difficult to replace. The remainder of the track was disposed of by British Rail, the society's intention being to reinstate it as funds permit. The Kinneil & Manuel Light Railway Order, made on 5 April 1988, authorised British Rail to transfer the line to the Bo'ness & Kinneil Railway Co. Ltd., and that company to lease it to the Scottish Railway Preservation Society.

By 1988 the track had been replaced (but not finally aligned or levelled) as far as Birkhill, $3\frac{1}{2}$ miles from Bo'ness. Here a new station was being built, and here, formerly, was Birkhill clay mine which is being preserved by the Bo'ness Heritage Trust and is mentioned in chapter twelve. But the railway was not re-opened that year to Birkhill, as had been anticipated, because unexpected events elsewhere absorbed all available effort.

Late in 1987 British Rail Property Board sold the site of Falkirk depot for development and the SRPS had to move out in a hurry. The sweetener was that British Rail, which had been very reluctant to re-instate the connection to the branch at Bo'ness Junction – this had previously taken the form of facing points out of a line traversed by frequent fast trains – was now prepared to put in a connection in the form of trailing points and a headshunt. This in turn meant that it was possible to envisage through steam excursions between Edinburgh, Stirling and Bo'ness.

What it meant immediately, however, was that the stock at Falkirk had to be evacuated. A new base was found at Perth for the coaches used for railtours over British Rail – by then a set of British Railways mark one coaches had been acquired – and two locomotives, two wagons, a station building and some lesser items went for display at Glasgow Garden Festival. (The station building, from Monifieth, was destined eventually for Birkhill). Almost everything else remaining at Falkirk, including four complete steam locomotives, four diesels, several coaches, substantial components such as bogies and boilers, and heavy plant, had to be moved to Bo'ness by road. The immediate consequence was acute congestion in the sidings, alleviated gradually as more storage sidings were laid. Even so, many historic vehicles were standing in the open.

The society already had plans to move the Penman Boilerworks building to Bo'ness – this 440 ft by 45 ft structure originated as the machinery hall at the 1888 Glasgow International Exhibition, after which it was moved to Dalmarnock and became for eighty years or so the Caledonian Boilerworks of Penman & Co, builders of stationary boilers. At Bo'ness it would become the museum building, and late in 1988 the society was appealing for funds to build a further reserve collection building, large enough to span three tracks and house fifteen bogie coaches.

To meet part of the cost, a grant of £18,000 had already been awarded by the Scottish Museums Council, one example of the generous but well-merited financial support the society has received from official bodies ranging from the local authorities to the Scottish Tourist Board and the Historic Buildings Council.

With such support to match their own efforts, the 900 members of the Scottish Railway Preservation Society were able to achieve their delayed goal of re-opening to Birkhill, at Easter 1989. In choosing this little branch line to represent steam railways in all Scotland, the society perhaps chose more aptly than it knew: from the high ground above Birkhill one looks out – on a fine day – across farmland, through which the railway runs, to the Firth of Forth, the industries of Grangemouth and the hills of Perthshire in the distance. The scene is Scotland in microcosm.

# CHAPTER FOUR

# *P S* WAVERLEY *AND THE* PADDLE STEAMER PRESERVATION SOCIETY

*STEAMERS ON THE CLYDE*

*D*uring the summer of 1968, while British Rail was busily withdrawing the last of its standard gauge steam locomotives, its subsidiary the Caledonian Steam Packet Co. Ltd continued to employ four steamships – two paddle steamers and two turbine steamers – in its fleet of fourteen ships on the Firth of Clyde. Clyde passenger shipping had declined a bit over the years, but nevertheless British Rail's booklet describing the Clyde Coast steamer services (sic) for that summer makes interesting reading. The cover featured the double arrow logo as well as a paddle box and wheel, and the booklet needed sixty six pages to provide details of all the services, cruises, tours and excursions on offer. Some vessels carried motor vehicles, drive-on, drive-off, but many including the steamships did not: the steamships tended to be used on the long distance cruising routes. Just as they had for generations, ships connected with trains at Craigendoran and Fairlie Pier as well as Gourock and Wemyss Bay, and served destinations as far off as Campbeltown, Inveraray and Arrochar as well as the islands, and the resorts on the north shore of the firth.

It was a swansong. Change as radical as that on the railways proper was about to come to the Clyde steamer services. The Transport Act 1968, in the course of making widespread reforms in transport throughout Britain, established the Scottish Transport Group, and transferred to it the nationalised bus undertakings in Scotland together with the Caledonian Steam Packet Co. Ltd, with effect from 1 January 1969. The transfer brought CSP's operations under the accountants' microscope, and what they found, as reported in Scottish Transport Group accounts for 1969, its first year of operation, was: Road Passenger Transport, turnover £28,998,000, profit £1,882,000; Shipping companies, turnover £3,437,000, loss £265,000. The actual loss of Caledonian Steam Packet Co. Ltd. had increased from £87,000 in 1968 to £272,000 in 1969 – the different figure for the loss by 'shipping companies' takes into account a subsidy to David MacBrayne Ltd, at that date half-owned by STG. (Later it was wholly absorbed, and the name of the shipping company changed to Caledonian MacBrayne in 1973.)

Cruising, the accompanying annual report for 1969 noted particularly, was loss-making: and although it was not the company's intention to suppress it, cruising was to be encouraged only where consistent with economical use of ships. And what the new group intended to do was to transfer as much traffic as possible from traditional ships to car and vehicle ferries. Three years later the government reinforced this attitude, announcing a policy decision that sea services to Scottish islands should be modernised by conversion to roll-on, roll-off ferries by 'the shortest practicable sea crossings'. Under railway control, Clyde shipping services had been longitudinal, down the firth as extensions of railway routes. The new operator had no such constraint: Clyde shipping services became lateral ones, ferries traversing the shortest crossings in the interests of road transport. One cannot help but wonder, too, whether it was not very much in the commercial interest of the new group to carry passengers from, say, Campbeltown all the way to Glasgow by bus, rather than to take them by ship to Fairlie Pier and there hand them over to British Rail. At any rate there was a great reduction in the quantity and extent of services on the Clyde.

No doubt growing prosperity which had led to the increasing popularity of holidays abroad and motor cars at home had made change inevitable. Probably it was overdue. But sudden change is harsh. In 1977 Caledonian MacBrayne withdrew its last Clyde steamship, the turbine steamer *Queen Mary II*, and in its annual report for 1980 stated that it would withdraw from Clyde Cruising after the end of the 1980 season, although in practice this decision has not been put totally into effect. However the tradition of pleasure cruises down the Firth of Clyde by steamer, by then more than one and a half centuries old, came periously close to total collapse. That it survived was due to the preservation of the paddle steamer *Waverley* by the Paddle Steamer Preservation Society in 1974.

*T*he Paddle Steamer Preservation Society had been formed in England in 1959. It was then already evident that paddle steamers, a familiar feature of the British seaside, were declining rapidly in numbers and risked becoming extinct. In 1967, after some false starts, the society successfully purchased for preservation the 108 ft long paddle steamer *Kingswear Castle*, the last paddle steamer on the River Dart. She was taken to the River Medway for overhaul and restoration, but progress was very slow. In 1969 the Scottish Branch of the society was formed.

In 1973 it became clear that the career of PS *Waverley*, by then the last paddle steamer in the Caledonian MacBrayne fleet, was drawing to a close. She was said to be losing £100,000 a year. Douglas McGowan, PSPS Scottish Branch secretary, was invited to CalMac head office: he expected to be told she was to be withdrawn. What he got was an offer to sell the ship to the society for the sum of £1.00. Caledonian MacBrayne was not unconscious of its heritage. When the purchase was eventually made, Scottish Transport Group chairman Sir Patrick Thomas donated £1.00 to the society to cover its cost.

PS *Waverley*, 240 feet long, 693 gross tons, had been ordered by the London & North Eastern Railway in 1945. The LNER had lost two of its fleet of five Clyde paddle vessels during the Second World War, a previous PS *Waverley* having been sunk at Dunkirk. Even in the late 1940s, paddle steamers had, for the Clyde, specific advantages over more modern types of vessel: they featured shallow draught, which was important particularly at Craigendoran where the LNER ships were based, and the ability to stop quickly by putting the paddles astern, which helped time-keeping on rail-connected services with frequent pier calls.

The new paddle steamer was built by A & J Inglis Ltd at Pointhouse, and launched on 2 October 1946; she was then towed to Greenock where her engine and boiler, made by Rankin & Blackmore Ltd, were installed. The original boiler of double-ended Scotch type had six furnaces and produced steam at 180 lb per sq. in. The engine, which still drives the ship, is triple-expansion, its three cylinders laid out across the hull to drive directly on to the paddle shaft. Cylinder dimensions are: diameters, high pressure, 24 in., intermediate pressure 39 in., low pressure 66 in; stroke 66 in. A remarkable photographic record of her construction survives, and has been published by the PSPS as *Birth of a Legend*. As one sees her hull taking shape in the Clydeside murk, it does not need much imagination to realise how pleasant it must have been for those working on her, after six wartime years, to turn to building a vessel of a type synonymous with happy peacetime summer days.

Certainly her first route, when she entered service in the summer of 1947, was from Craigendoran up Loch Long to Arrochar. Her subsequent career was typical rather than exceptional. She passed through successive changes of ownership imposed by nationalisation, her boiler was converted to burn oil in1957, and she operated over many of the well-known routes for Clyde steamers. But she turned out to have been the last paddle steamer built for service there, and by 1970 she was the last survivor.

It seems likely that when Caledonian MacBrayne first considered selling *Waverley* to the PSPS for a nominal sum, they envisaged that the ship would be preserved as a static museum, and there were those in the society who favoured this course. Happily those who wished to attempt to keep her operating prevailed, though this was a huge undertaking for the Scottish branch of the society with, then, fewer than 300 members. (Today membership is around 700.)

To own and operate the ship required a limited company distinct from the society itself. A ready-made company was acquired and its name changed in April 1974 to Waverley Steam Navigation Co. Ltd. Formally, its principal objects are to carry on business as shipowners, and to organise and conduct trips and excursions. All directors must be members of the PSPS, and the only shareholders are directors and former directors.

WAVERLEY  BACK  IN  SERVICE

*P*S *Waverley* changed hands on 8 August 1974. The first need was to fit her for cruising again. A public appeal for funds raised over £40,000, the Scottish Tourist Board added £30,000, Glasgow Corporation donated £11,000. *Waverley* was drydocked for survey and repairs early in 1975. She returned to public service on 22 May 1975, under the command of Capt. D.L. Neill who has continued to be her captain from that day to this. Caledonian MacBrayne in the sale agreement had not only reserved the right to re-purchase the ship should Waverley Steam Navigation Co. be unable to operate her, but also imposed the condition that she should not be operated in competition with its own ships. The effect was that for her first season *Waverley* was based alternately at Ayr and at Glasgow itself. None the less more than 121,000 passengers sailed in her and although

PS *Waverley* is drydocked for survey and overhaul.          DR. J. McKENDRICK

she operated at a loss, the results were encouraging enough to suggest that the ship did have a future ahead of her.

With the passage of time this has been confirmed to be correct, and the ship has operated every summer since, although there have been some nasty moments. The nastiest came on 15 July 1977, when *Waverley* went aground on the Gantock Rocks off Dunoon. This meant repairs in drydock, so that she was out of service for seven weeks at the busiest part of the season. The effect on the finances was that the operating loss for the season, after crediting subsidies, went up from £9,887 in 1976 to £65,752 in 1977. It was 1982 before a surplus was achieved after crediting subsidies.

One means by which the results were improved was to extend both the operating season and the cruising range of the vessel. The two are inter-related. Summer on the Clyde is all too short, and maintaining ships for use only during a short season had been one of the factors which made Clyde cruising uneconomic. In the late spring of 1977, centenary celebrations for Llandudno pier prompted *Waverley* to visit Liverpool and the North Wales coast, and to offer cruises while there. That was but one of many parts of the coast of Britain where paddle steamers, once familiar, had seemingly become only a memory. The results were encouraging enough for a further southward venture to be made during April and May 1978, and *Waverley* visited the South Coast and the Thames, sailing from Tower Pier, London. This visit became the precedent for further successful visits South, and in the spring of 1981 the visit was extended so that *Waverley* for the first time circumnavigated Great Britain before returning to the Clyde.

So a cruising pattern became established in which *Waverley* spends some weeks in spring, and also in autumn, cruising on waters away from the Clyde. In this way she has visited the West Coast of Scotland, Dublin and the Isle of Man among many other localities. In 1984 when visiting the Medway she was able to rendezvous for the first time with PS *Kingswear Castle*, restored to working order largely through enthusiasm brought about by *Waverley's* success; and her success in perpetuating cruising in the Bristol Channel made it possible to obtain the 1949-built MV *Balmoral*, which had operated there until 1980, and put her back into service in 1986 to offer a full summer season of cruises.

By 1978 *Waverley's* boiler was beginning to show its age – plates were becoming thin and that July she was out of service for two weeks due to cracks in old welds in the casing. It was also inefficient in a time of high fuel costs. During the winter of 1980 a new 'Steambloc' boiler was ordered from Babcock Power Ltd, Renfrew. This is a standard type used in industry, of welded construction and with both fire and water tubes.

New boiler is lowered into PS *Waverley* in March 1981.                    DEREK PETERS

The new boiler was installed in *Waverley* in March 1981. That noted Glasgow landmark, the Finnieston crane, which was later to become famous for its suspension of a straw locomotive, was used to lift out the old boiler and insert the new. The old boiler now belongs to the Royal Museums of Scotland and can be seen where it is stored at Bo'ness station, Bo'ness & Kinneil Railway.

*Waverley*'s new boiler, by the time it had been installed, cost some £200,000. Much of this was raised by members of the PSPS, and grants were made by the Scottish Tourist Board and local authorities. Once it was in use, the fuel bill was reduced by 17 per cent. But the boiler has not proved entirely satisfactory in service. Towards the end of the 1982 season it was found that sediment was building up and blocking the tubes, because of a design fault which Babcock corrected during the ship's winter refit. Then in July 1987 a major fault appeared in the form of a bulge in the floor of a furnace. This was repaired by Babcock but after a fortnight the problem re-appeared and the ship's passenger certificate was withdrawn by the Department of Trade – an action with which the Waverley SN Co. was in the circumstances happy to concur. Possible causes of the over-heating which produced the fault are thought to have been a misaligned burner and/or a new water softener causing oil to be deposited on the metal. PSPS members raised £50,000 to pay for repairs: these were put out to tender and in due course the contract awarded to N.E.I. Thompson Cochran of Annan; the work included cutting out and replacing two sections of each furnace, complete overhaul of the burners and installation of thermocouples to give early warning of any overheating. The ship re-entered service on 1 May 1988, and completed the season without further boiler problems.

Yet problems with the boiler are but one aspect of the problems associated with maintaining a large vintage paddle steamer. *Waverley* has to be drydocked annually for survey by Department of Trade surveyor: yet with the decline of Clyde shipbuilding there is now only one drydock left on the Clyde which is wide enough to take her. In 1988 she was drydocked at Milford Haven, the voyage there providing a convenient trial run after boiler repairs. Even the timber from which the paddle wheel floats were originally made, American Rock Elm, has now become a protected species, so that replacement floats (11 ft long, 3 ft broad and 3 in. thick) are made from the African hardwood Iroko.

The Department of Trade requires that all the ship's crew should be fully qualified – from captain, mate and engineer to deck crew, and even stewards who have basic life saving certificates. So the ship's summer-season crew of thirty three are all full-time paid staff. Volunteers from the PSPS assist aboard in the souvenir shop in summer and help with maintenance in the winter. They also do a great deal of publicity ashore, and when the ship calls at certain piers, such as Helensburgh, volunteers take the ropes when she comes alongside. The arrangements for this vital task vary from pier to pier according to its ownership – at Largs and Brodick for instance arrangements are made for CalMac staff to take the ropes.

Cruising and day-to-day operation of the ship are now the responsibility of Waverley Excursions Ltd, subsidiary of Waverley Steam Navigation Co. Ltd. incorporated in 1980 'to carry on in Scotland and elsewhere the business of pleasure steamer operators'. The ship is chartered to Waverley Excursions Ltd by Waverley SN Co. Ltd, which remains the owner, carries out the winter refit and obtains her passenger-carrying certificate from the Department of Trade. Ownership, and with it the long-term future of the *Waverley*, are thus protected from the financial risks inherent in daily operation. It is hoped that Waverley SN Co. Ltd will be able to achieve charitable status, and the Paddle Steamer Preservation Society has become both a registered charity and a company limited by guarantee.

Wherever *Waverley* cruises at the beginning and end of the season, it remains the policy that she should spend the July and August peak season on the Clyde. The author took the opportunity during 1988 one day to join her at Helensburgh – to go aboard there was fortuitously appropriate, to join the last Clyde paddle steamer at the place where that strange man Henry Bell planned the first, and to see a little way upstream the remains of Craigendoran pier at which *Waverley* was originally based. Following Craigendoran's closure, the approach to Helensburgh pier was dredged in 1979 for *Waverley* to call there.

Aboard *Waverley* are traditional paddle steamer delights, small and large – from cane chairs which date from the ship's construction in one of the saloons, and haddock & chips in the restaurant (self-service, now), to a fascinating close-up view of the paddles when, with the ship moored at destination, a door in the side of the hull is opened for an engineer to climb out on to the paddle wheel to inspect it – and, above all, the gallery round the engine room which enables passengers to observe that massive engine at work. And then to cruise to Tighnabruaich and back, calling at Dunoon and Rothesay, was to travel a real Clyde steamer route – impossible by land but straightforward by water, linking places which once grew and prospered because of steamer communication. Here, *Waverley* seems so much at one with her surroundings that it is a shock suddenly to recollect that of course there are not going to be half a dozen more paddle steamers round the next bend, and she really is the sole survivor.

# $S$ TEAM
# $O$ N
# $B$ RITISH
# $R$ AIL

## *THE WEST HIGHLAND SCENE*

$W$ith needless warning whistle, and rail-resounding wheels,' wrote Sassoon, and Rolt borrowed the verse to introduce *Railway Adventure*, his account of the first preserved railway, '"That train's quite like an old familiar friend", one feels'.

Standing beneath a dripping oak tree on the south side of Loch Eil on a day of driving rain, I was reminded of the couplet by the whistle of K1 2-6-0 no. 2005. It is very shrill, and sounded frequently, though probably much needed. The Mallaig steam train was drifting along the north side of the loch; abruptly, the locomotive blew off, then as abruptly the escaping steam ceased as the driver opened the regulator for the climb to Glenfinnan and beyond, smoke and steam from the exhaust now mingling with the mist, till only the exhaust beat remained and eventually that too faded.

A summer already wetter than usual had excelled itself by producing a south-westerly gale to accompany a downpour. Earlier, attempting to photograph the K1 raising steam in Fort William goods yard, I had been obliged to shelter in the lee of the end of the support coach while, as I discovered later, the Ben Nevis hill race was being called off and competitors suffering from exposure helicoptered from the summit. I gave up and, photography abandoned, resolved to enjoy the spectacle of a steam train in bad weather in the 1980s. It was, in this instance, an SRPS special which had originated from Edinburgh. Hence my position in the limited shelter provided by the oak tree.

At any rate I hope that to those along the way the regular steam train from Fort William to Mallaig has once again become an old familiar friend. Of course, had I been writing this in the late 1960s rather than the late 1980s the position would have been quite different. Then the likelihood that, two decades later, one would be watching a steam train on that route (or quite possibly any train at all) would have seemed like cloud-cuckooland.

*C*ertainly when British Railways withdrew the last of its standard gauge steam locomotives in 1968, it then banned privately-owned steam locomotives from its tracks. This was a great inconvenience to John B. Cameron. For Cameron, in 1966, had purchased, on her withdrawal by BR, A4 class streamlined 4-6-2 no. 60009 *Union of South Africa.*

A4 Pacific *Union of South Africa* halts at Larbert on 27 April 1985 with (left to right) SRPS train organiser Douglas Hodgkins, John B. Cameron, Locomotive Inspector Louis Gracie of Edinburgh.                    BRIAN DOBBS

Forth Bridge centenary will be celebrated in 1990; here it dwarfs A4 no. nine and train as they cross it in 1985.

BILL ROBERTON

Of all the A4s that survived until 1966, no. 60009 was in the best condition. Her swansong, and that of some others of the class, had been on accelerated expresses between Glasgow and Aberdeen, but they had been built for the principal East Coast Route expresses between King's Cross and Scotland. *Union of South Africa* was built by the LNER in 1937 and at first called *Osprey* (many of the class were named after birds) but within a few months she and four sisters were renamed after the dominions, prior to being set to haul the *Coronation* express. This high speed train was put on between London and Edinburgh to celebrate the coronation of King George VI.

The locomotive had a distinguished career, regularly hauling the royal train during the 1950s and becoming the last steam locomotive overhauled at Doncaster, in 1963. J.B. Cameron bought her, together with the tender from sister locomotive 60004 (her own tender was defective), for about £3,000. On 25 March 1967 she then hauled a steam farewell excursion, arranged by BR and so popular that it had to be made up to eighteen coaches. But it was not to become a precedent: instead, steam was banned.

About this time John B. Cameron, who was and is a farmer on a large scale with several farms, had bought Lochty Farm in Fife as an agricultural investment. Across it ran the last mile and a half of rural branch line, the East Fife Central Railway, closed eighteen months before by British Railways. The penny dropped. He was able to buy it, with such track as remained (more was bought subsequently), a shed was built, and *Nine*, as 60009 was known among railwaymen, transferred there by road. On 14 June 1967 the Lochty Private Railway was inaugurated. That first season, *Nine* ran up and down only as a light engine; later, coaches were obtained and passengers carried.

There is more about the Lochty Railway in chapter six. As for steam on main lines, it was five long years before British Rail relented and agreed to allow a limited number of excursions, operated by preserved steam locomotives, on specified routes, usually secondary main lines. One of the first routes specified was Dundee-Thornton Junction-Dunfermline-Inverkeithing-Kirkcaldy-Thornton Junction, and on 3 April 1973 no. 60009 was taken by road from Lochty and put back on BR metals at Ladybank. On 5 May she successfully hauled the first steam excursion in Scotland following the lifting of the ban, and over the next few years, specials operated by her became a regular part of the Scottish railway scene. Her most usual routes became Edinburgh to Dundee and Aberdeen, and Edinburgh-Stirling-Perth-Ladybank, the latter junction being between Edinburgh and Dundee. But on occasion she reached both Inverness and Ayr under her own steam, and in 1985 worked a special by Dumfries, Carlisle, Settle and Leeds to York, where she went on display at the National Railway Museum for some three months and powered regular steam specials to Scarborough.

No. 60009's normal base was established at Markinch, in a shed which had been a parcels depot and offered appropriate security. A small workshop has been built up, staffed by volunteers to whom maintaining *Nine* is a labour of love, and five minutes journey away is Thornton triangle, where the locomotive can conveniently be turned. In 1987 *Nine's* seven-year certificate to run on British Rail expired, and although she came in from her last run in good order, a major overhaul involving lifting the boiler and replacing crown stays over the firebox was needed before she can be certificated again. As I write this, her owner is making plans for the work to be done, with a view to the celebrations proposed for the centenary of the Forth Bridge in 1990. And about the same time J.B. Cameron was appointed both chairman of British Rail's Scottish Railway Board, and a part-time member of the main British Railways Board: which sound like positions with interesting potential for a steam locomotive owner. With all this, it is sad to learn that the name *Union of South Africa*, given to the locomotive in good faith at a time of national rejoicing, today has practical disadvantages. Should re-naming become desirable, there would be an element of appropriateness in reverting to her original name *Osprey*: by happy coincidence it is that of a species once common in Scotland, which became virtually extinct, and then re-appeared.

*STEAM RAILTOURS*

*T*he Scottish Railway Preservation Society has a long tradition of organising excursions over British Rail using its own coaches (diesel-hauled during the steam ban and for the most part subsequently) although the historic coaches originally used have now given way to a set of British Railways mark I coaches: it was these that formed the train mentioned at the start of this chapter. Nor was the steam ban enforced quite so rigidly in Scotland as further south – I recollect the glee of SRPS officials when, although the ban was at its height, a new addition to their collection – an industrial saddle-tank locomotive – was delivered to the Falkirk depot over BR under its own steam.

Eventually, SRPS steam locomotives were able to return on occasion to BR tracks. No. 419 and *Morayshire* took part in the 1975 cavalcade of locomotives on the Stockton & Darlington Railway to mark its 150th anniversary, and in 1979 for instance 419 ran under her own steam from Falkirk to Glasgow Central for exhibition. A greater achievement came in 1980 when *Maude* went south, under her own steam and hauling two restored Caledonian Railway coaches, to Rainhill for the 150th anniversary celebrations of the Liverpool & Manchester Railway. The same year both *Maude* and *Morayshire* worked special passenger trains over British Rail – this was a useful precedent for both locomotives were much smaller than the steam locomotives BR was generally allowing on to the main line, having a big engine policy to maximise revenue from steam specials. The author was happy to chair the sub-committee of the Association of Railway Preservation Societies which decided that year that the SRPS should receive the association's annual award. This is made to a society which has made an outstanding contribution to railway preservation.

Subsequently *Maude* operated widely over BR in Scotland, notably round the Edinburgh Suburban Line (long closed to regular passenger traffic) at Christmastime with 'Santa Specials', and to Bathgate in 1986 to mark re-opening of that branch to passenger trains.

In 1981 and 1982 the Strathspey Railway's class 5 4-6-0 no. 5025, mentioned in chapter six, operated steam specials between Perth and Aviemore, and between Inverness and Kyle of Lochalsh. These operations were sadly ended by the locomotive's recurrent firebox troubles. But in 1984 British Rail took up an idea which had been put to it, and instituted a regular timetabled steam train service over the $41\frac{1}{2}$ miles of the West Highland Railway extension from Fort William to Mallaig. Initially an experiment, it has, says BR, been an outstanding success. *Maude* was among the locomotives used at first, mostly on short trains between Fort William and Glenfinnan only. Larger locomotives, usually of class five, have been used on the heavier trains making the full journey. During 1988 the locomotives used have been K1 class 2-6-0 no. 2005, built by British Railways to LNER design, and LMS class five 4-6-0 no. 5305 *Alderman A.E. Draper*; during the height of the summer season the train made a return journey from Fort William to Mallaig on Mondays, Tuesdays, Thursdays and Sundays (less frequently at the beginning and end of the season) – and on Sundays it provided the only public transport between Fort William and Mallaig.

The continuing progress of modernisation of British Rail, while thoroughly desirable from most points of view, has the regrettable side-effect of rendering the system less and less suitable for steam locomo-

From time to time steam excursions bring locomotives to Scotland which are normally based in the South. Here LMS Jubilee class 4-6-0 *Leander* leaves Edinburgh Waverley on 30 March 1985.                     BILL ROBERTON

West Highland weather, as encountered by the author: in a gale accompanied by a torrential downpour, K1 2-6-0 no. 2005 prepares to leave Fort William with an SRPS special train from Edinburgh to Mallaig on 3 September 1988. Steam impresses, whatever the conditions.                     AUTHOR

Class five 4-6-0 no. 5305 crosses the Caledonian Canal at Banavie en route for Mallaig on a truly summery 31 July 1988.

JOHN LECK

tives. One of the causes of the steam ban was the elimination of facilities for servicing steam locomotives. Ingenuity could overcome some of these problems, given the will, by for instance obtaining locomotive water supplies from hydrant or hose or even, at Achnasheen on the Kyle line, by portable pump from a convenient burn. But the line from Edinburgh to Aberdeen, for long the stamping ground of 60009, is no longer available for steam locomotives: its upgrading for High Speed Trains has meant increased superelevation and reduced clearances, and the turntable at Aberdeen Ferryhill has been removed. Nor are steam specials over the Edinburgh Suburban Line likely to survive electrification of the eastern section of the route, between Waverley and Portobello, in 1989. So the routes available for steam specials in Scotland are, as I write in late 1988, principally those of the central belt – Edinburgh-Glasgow-Perth – together with Fort William-Mallaig and the Glasgow & South Western line via Kilmarnock to Carlisle. The latter route in particular is traversed by spring and autumn specials hauled by locomotives en route between their bases in the North of England and Fort William. Southbound in autumn, these locomotives also haul specials over the West Highland line between Fort William and Craigendoran. The northbound run in the spring is made tender-first and therefore light engine: no turntable survives at Fort William (or Mallaig) and Mallaig to Fort William is regarded as about the maximum run for a train hauled tender-first.

Steam specials over British Rail are the responsibility of its InterCity sector. On BR, the sectors – InterCity, Provincial, Network SouthEast – are responsible for specification of services, infrastructure, rolling stock and marketing of services. The regions – Scottish Region and so on – are responsible for actual day-to-day operation of the railway. The analogy, in manufacturing industry, would be planning and production. So the Fort William-Mallaig steam train is an InterCity responsibility, although the line otherwise is a Provincial one. For this service, BR hires the locomotives from their owners – no. 2005 for instance is owned by the North Eastern Locomotive Preservation Group. BR provides train crew, coaches and coal. Railways have a tradition of long service, and there are still based at Fort William sufficient drivers, who were passed to drive locomotives in the days of steam, to operate the Mallaig steam train; but firemen are being trained anew on the job. Each locomotive owner remains responsible for preparation and disposal of the locomotive, maintenance and repairs.

Arrangements for steam specials elsewhere are similar, except that it is normally the tour operator who charters the locomotive from its owner, and arranges with British Rail to run the train. The Steam Locom-

North British Railway 0-6-0 *Maude* approaches Birkhill, Bo'ness & Kinneil Railway, in September 1988. TV cameraman is travelling on the cab steps. AUTHOR

Despite its authentic appearance, Bo'ness station has been built since 1979 by the Scottish Railway Preservation Society. Old buildings and materials have been re-used. AUTHOR

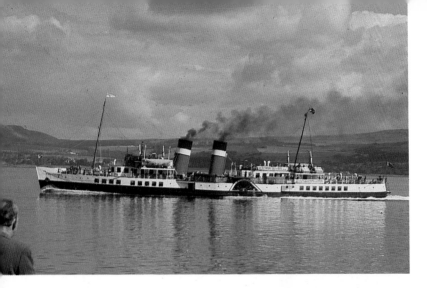

Paddle steamer *Waverley* passes Port Glasgow. NORMAN BURNISTON PHOTOGRAPHY

Class five 4-6-0 no. 5305 heads south over the West Highland line, between Bridge of Orchy and Tyndrum, on 17 October 1987 after a summer's operation on Mallaig steam trains. JOHN LECK

Santa special circles the Edinburgh Suburban line on 13 December 1987.   JOHN LECK

K1 class 2-6-0 no. 2005 hauls a Fort William-Mallaig train near Glenfinnan on
4 October 1987.

JOHN LECK

Class five 4-6-0 no. 44871, owned and overhauled by a Scottish group, undergoes a steam test at Carnforth in 1988 — her first time in steam for ten years.

P. VAN CAMPENHOUT

Boat of Garten, Strathspey Railway, in 1981, with class five 4-6-0 no. 5025 ready to leave for Aviemore.

AUTHOR

Miniature Rio Grande 2-8-2 crosses one of the viaducts on the $7\frac{1}{4}$ in. gauge railway at the House of Ross, Comrie, Perthshire, in September 1988. AUTHOR

Two-foot gauge 0-4-2 tank locomotive *Saccharine* is seen here at Alford station, 26 June 1988. AUTHOR

SS *Sir Walter Scott* leaves Trossachs Pier, Loch Katrine in September 1988.    AUTHOR

SS *Vic 32* enters the sea lock on the Crinan Canal at Ardrishaig on 8 August 1988.

AUTHOR

Steam Yacht *Ocean Mist* is now static at Leith as a restaurant, but the engine room still contains its triple expansion engine and there are plans to open it to the public.

AUTHOR

The *Craigievar Express*, built by a village postman in 1895, runs its own steam at the Grampian Transport Museum, Alford, on 26 June 1988.

AUTHOR

Road steamers parade at the Grampian Transport Museum, Alford, on 26 June 1988, a steam power activity Sunday.                                    AUTHOR

Smoke from a wee pug, the Scottish Mining Museum's Grant Ritchie 0-4-2 tank locomotive, billows round Prestongrange beam engine house on 3 July 1988.

AUTHOR

otive Operators' Association co-ordinates runs and routes, and negotiates with BR on behalf of owners.

*4 4 8 7 1*

*O*wners who wish to have their
locomotives certificated to run on British Rail have to meet stringent BR
requirements relating to both the boiler and its mountings, and the
mechanical part of the locomotive, with inspections made by a central
inspectorate based in Derby. Locomotive no. 44871 will provide a good
example. She is one of the numerous LMS class 5 4-6-0s, and was built in
1945, although the boiler now fitted is older, probably dating from 1937:
the LMS policy of standardisation meant that when locomotives were
overhauled, components were moved from one to another. At any rate,
her moment of fame came in 1968. On Saturday 11 August British Rail
ran the last steam train hauled by its own locomotives over standard
gauge track. This was the 'Fifteen-Guinea Special' – strange that the fare
should have been quoted in those particular pre-decimalisation terms
soon to follow the working steam locomotive into virtual oblivion – and
it ran from Liverpool to Manchester and Carlisle and back via the Settle
& Carlisle line. No. 44871 was one of the four locomotives which hauled
it over part of its journey, and among the many who gathered to watch
her go by was Graham Ellis (who was later to be one of the promoters of
the Mull railway). After the last run, she was kept in steam over the rest of
the weekend, becoming the last BR standard gauge locomotive in steam
so that the act of dropping the fire could be filmed on the Monday by the
BBC – a film which I understand was subsequently destroyed!

However no. 44871 was purchased for preservation at Steamtown,
Carnforth, Lancashire, and with eventual relaxation of the steam ban
returned to use on specials such as the Cumbrian Coast Express. She
was named *Sovereign* to mark the Queen's Silver Jubilee in 1977, but in
1978 a corroded boiler tube burst while she was raising steam, and she
was taken out of traffic pending an overhaul, which was a long time
coming.

It was eventually taken in hand by a Scottish group headed by Graham Ellis, Douglas Buchan, Willie Johnstone and, as chief engineer,
John Allan who had been helping to look after *Maude* while she was
running on the main line. Arrangements were formalised: the owners,
by 1988 Willie Johnstone with a two-thirds share and Graham Ellis with

one-third, had leased the locomotive for a nominal rent to the 44871 'Sovereign' Preservation Group which was incorporated as a company limited by guarantee in 1986.

The locomotive was stripped down at Carnforth the same year and the boiler moved to Airdrie where covered accommodation was available and the team set about re-tubing, de-scaling, renewing firebox stays, and other tasks, all in consultation with BR's boiler inspector. The team has been described to me as 'one engineer and seven assistants': but while to most of us a steam locomotive boiler seems, at close quarters, both very substantial and awesome in the steam pressure it contains, the assistants were fortunate in that in their engineer they had a man with long experience of power station engineering, so that 44871's boiler seemed comparatively puny in both size and the pressures involved. Consequently the boiler passed both hydraulic pressure and steam tests under BR supervision early in 1988, and was then returned to Carnforth to be re-united with the frames which had been receiving a full mechanical overhaul by members of the group. Within only a few weeks the locomotive was re-assembled and in steam; in October she went to North East England to have worn wheels re-profiled on BR's wheel lathe at Thornaby, Cleveland, and successfully hauled an eight-coach test train. After this she returned to Carnforth, and it is anticipated that no. 44871 will be hauling trains between Fort William and Mallaig during the summer of 1989.

# $S$TANDARD
# $G$AUGE
# $R$AILWAY
# $P$RESERVATION

## THE STRATHSPEY RAILWAY

$W$ith nearly five miles of standard gauge railway open from Aviemore to Boat of Garten, and plans to rebuild a further seven miles to Grantown-on-Spey at an estimated cost around £2 million, the Strathspey Railway is the most ambitious undertaking of its sort in Scotland. There are preserved railways in England which may have even greater ambitions, but the Strathspey is probably the furthest from centres of population, and has the most extreme climate, for it is far to the north and lies about 800 feet above sea level, with all that that implies in maintenance difficulties and extra cost.

Nevertheless, to those who in the late 1960s continued the Strathspey Railway project independently of the Scottish Railway Preservation Society (the origin of the scheme has been mentioned in chapter three) the Aviemore to Boat of Garten line had a lot going for it. It was, and is, of manageable length, easily graded, lacking sharp curves and with few civil engineering structures to demand expensive maintenance. It has fine views of the Cairngorms too. The Highlands & Islands Development Board continued to offer support, keen to encourage diversification in the range of attractions for visitors to the booming resort of Aviemore, particularly outside the ski-ing season, and Aviemore is easy of access from the South by both road and rail.

The Strathspey Railway Co. Ltd. was incorporated on 5 August 1971, its principal objects being 'to purchase ... from the Board of British Railways the existing railway line from Aviemore to Boat of Garten' and to 'restore, equip, maintain and work' it. It is also empowered to extend by purchasing 'adjoining railway lines and the sites of abandoned lines'.

The original subscribers included W.E.C. Watkinson who became the railway's greatest individual benefactor until his sad death in 1981, Eric Cooper who was for many years chairman, and Douglas Barclay who with wife Catherine took part in the first volunteer working party. Douglas has now been joint managing director and company secretary since the company was formed, and Catherine is a director and assistant secretary.

The original authorised capital was £10,000 in £1 shares, but the limit has been raised at intervals and by late 1988 a total of £112,500 had been raised by issue of shares, much of it by means of successive rights issues to existing shareholders. The company is not a public limited company and so had not issued a prospectus inviting the public to subscribe – but the number of shareholders had grown gradually to reach 178. Many shareholders work on the railway as volunteers – no dividend is paid or anticipated, and profits are ploughed back. Among the shareholdings are four particularly large ones. The W.E.C. Watkinson Trust held 21,000 shares in 1988: this charitable trust was established under the terms of that gentleman's will to inherit his shareholding, together with his former LMS class five locomotive no. 5025, and certain pieces of rolling stock. A further 14,000 shares (in round figures) were held by the Strathspey Railway Trust; this was set up during Mr Watkinson's lifetime but since it had been unable to achieve charitable status it was expected that its shareholding would be transferred to the Watkinson Trust. The Strathspey Railway Association held over 19,000 shares; it was formed in 1972 to support the company in restoring, running and maintaining the railway and by 1988 had about 640 members. Most of the other shareholdings are comparatively small, with the exception of the 7,750 shares held by the Highlands & Islands Development Board. The support of the HIDB was vital in the early stages of the project: it loaned £22,000 towards the £44,250 purchase price of the line (a loan now almost entirely repaid) and provided a grant of £10,000 as well.

A contract was made in 1972 between the Strathspey Railway Co. and British Railways for purchase of the line. Strathspey supporters were able to start restoration work; on occasion trains were operated under BR supervision. After frustrating delays, 'The Strathspey Light Railway Order 1978' was made on 16 June of that year, transferring the line from BR to the Strathspey Railway Co. along with its statutory rights and liabilities and authorising its operation as a light railway. The LRO does more – it also covers the trackbed from Boat of Garten 'to a point 1 mile 100 yd north of Broomhill station' – well on the way to Grantown, that is – for the company by then had been able to purchase the trackbed for that section. Subsequently it has purchased the rest of the trackbed as far as Grantown.

The passenger train service started on 16 July 1978 between Boat of Garten and Aviemore, with five return trips, on Saturdays and Sundays and, during August, Tuesdays and Wednesdays also; it ran until 1 October. This pattern has become familiar, although the period of service has been steadily extended. In 1988 the train service operated, at weekends, from Easter until the end of October, and during the main summer season on every day of the week except Friday. In 1989 it is intended to run every day from 1 June until 30 September. On Friday evenings in summer, and some Saturday evenings too, there is *The Highlander* wine-and-dine special, with catering by the Boat Hotel, Boat of Garten and a lengthy pause among the heather for passengers to enjoy their meal. Once a week, too, the Royal Scotsman luxury tour train visits the Strathspey Railway, and spends the night in the quiet of Boat of Garten station.

It is able to do so because the connection between the Strathspey Railway and British Rail has been kept. To the good fortune of the Strathspey company, during the period when the Boat of Garten line was open to freight only, British Railways had altered the track layout at Aviemore so that what eventually became the Strathspey Railway no longer led to a passenger platform at Aviemore, but made an end-on connection with a goods siding. This has meant that the Strathspey Railway has been able to maintain physical connection with BR without the crippling charges which would have been implied by a connection direct into a main line. The bad news, back in 1972, was that British Railways was unwilling to allow Strathspey passenger trains access over its tracks into Aviemore passenger station, even had the layout permitted. National policy of the period towards preserved railways in general was reinforced at Aviemore by anticipation that all tracks would be needed for oil-boom traffic. The Strathspey Railway was faced with buying additional land and building its own station, Aviemore Speyside, a little way along its own line. Here there is at least space for an adequate car park, and the station looks a lot older-established than it is, for buildings and equipment have been brought from other sites in the Highlands and reconstructed here. The station building came from Dalnaspidal, the signal box from Garve, the footbridge from Longmorn, and the turntable from Kyle of Lochalsh.

The locomotive shed, on the other hand, is original, and large (four roads), dating from the period when Aviemore was an important junction. No longer in railway use, it was eventually made available in 1975. The tracks leading to it had been taken up, and had to be replaced: subsequently the shed has provided covered accommodation (much needed in a severe climate) for restoration, maintenance and storage of locomotives and rolling stock. Here a workshop has been established with equipment adequate for routine maintenance – radial drill, large and small lathes, large air compressor and so on. Boiler repairs are contracted out, much of the work being done (some of it on site) by Ian Storey Engineering of Morpeth, Northumberland.

By 1984 the roof of Aviemore shed, which had been in bad condition when the building was acquired, was letting in so much rain and snow that complete re-roofing was needed: an operation which cost £56,600 (more than the original cost of the railway!). Of this £18,000 was met by HIDB grant, and a further £16,500 by HIDB loan. Subsequently it was possible to provide a complete new electrical supply, suitable for a modern workshop, and stonework has been re-pointed by a Community Services programme.

The limitation on maintenance is available skilled manpower, for up here in the Highlands there is no reservoir of persons with heavy engineering skills, and in this department as in all others the railway is largely dependent on volunteers willing to come for a weekend or a week or more. There is a hard core of fifty or so regulars, and another fifty or so who come perhaps once a year. Until 1988 there was but one full-time employee, but it was anticipated that there would be two, and two part-time staff, in the summer of 1989.

Of the locomotives themselves, the line's large locomotive is no. 5025, built for the LMS in 1934 and one of the first of what was to become a highly successful class of mixed traffic locomotives. Many, including 5025, were used on the Highland Railway lines, and when she was eventually withdrawn she was purchased by W.E.C. Watkinson. She eventually arrived on the Strathspey Railway in 1975, and in due course hauled not only the Strathspey's own trains, but also in 1981 and 1982 steam specials over neighbouring British Rail routes. These are mentioned in chapter five. In 1983, however, she was found to have developed cracks in her firebox. Alternating attempts to cure such cracks by riveted and/or welded reinforcing plates, and the discovery of further cracks by ultra-sonic testing, have since been a continuing saga. The locomotive was used again in 1986, but she is, however, larger than is needed for the Strathspey Railway's own traffic, and uneconomic; probably her future lies in occasional use on publicised 'large engine days' which it is expected will be held during 1989.

Much more appropriate to the line's traffic – trains of four coaches are usual – are two small 2-6-0s of British Railways standard class two. One of these, no. 46464, was purchased on withdrawal by Ian Fraser who presented her to Dundee City Museums, which in turn loaned her to the Strathspey Railway. She was used on the first trains after re-opening in 1978, but her boiler is old and during the following year expensive repairs were found to be needed. Tasks which were more urgent took precedence, but in 1988 the company was negotiating with Dundee District Council to find out whether, if it provided a new firebox, the loan (which had expired) would be renewed. Speyside is a long way from Dundee, however, and it is possible the council may prefer the locomotive to return home to the locality in which she spent much of her working life.

As a matter of policy, none of the locomotives on the Strathspey Railway belongs to the railway company itself, which operates and maintains them by agreement with their owners. The railway company did, however, set up in 1975 a subsidiary company, the Highland Locomotive Company Ltd in which it maintains a 51 per cent interest, to acquire and provide locomotives. The second class two 2-6-0, no. 46512, is one of these acquisitions, but since she was acquired, like many other locomotives now in preservation, from Woodham Bros.' Barry scrapyard, her restoration to working order is proving a long drawn out process. Another of the subsidiary's locomotives though small, the 0-4-0 saddle tank *Clyde*, has been in recent seasons the reserve locomotive. Most trains, however, have been hauled by no. 60, a privately-owned 0-6-0 saddle tank of Austerity type. During 1987, no. 60 operated 99 per cent

Strathspey Railway's Austerity 0-6-0 saddle tank locomotive no. 60 is turned at Aviemore. Turntable was formerly at Kyle of Lochalsh.          BILL ROBERTON

Caledonian Railway 0-6-0 no. 828 stands inside Aviemore shed, Strathspey Railway, awaiting restoration to working order. BILL ROBERTON

of all Strathspey passenger train services, and ran 6,494 miles in the process. A new arrival in 1988, which is likely to share services in future with no. 60, is Bagnall 0-6-0 saddle tank *Victor* which was purchased privately from the West Somerset Railway.

Coaches which are used in regular passenger trains are for the most part British Railways mark I types, built in the 1950s. These belong to the railway company. The 1960 Pullman car *Amethyst*, which is included in the wine-and-dine trains, and other more historic coaches, including some of LMS origin, are privately owned.

The transfer of Caledonian Railway 0-6-0 no. 828 from Glasgow Museum of Transport to the Strathspey Railway was mentioned in chapter two. Her restoration to working order, financed by the Strathspey Railway Co. which is then entitled to ten years' use from her, was in 1988 approaching completion, and it was anticipated that both this locomotive and 46512 would be operating in the foreseeable future.

But these are not the only welcome developments anticipated. There are hopes once again that Strathspey trains may be able to enter Aviemore British Rail station. The problem here is not so much alteration of the track layout to suit, as the cost of altering the signalling. Even if they do eventually start from the BR station, Strathspey trains would probably continue to call at Aviemore Speyside, which would be more convenient for car-borne visitors. But more stimulating even than where Strathspey trains should start from is where they should go to. The original intent that the line should go to Grantown-on-Spey has always been the ambition, and in celebrating the tenth anniversary of its passenger services during 1988 the company announced plans to achieve that. The cost, as indicated above, seems at first sight astronomic. However the first section, just over four miles to Broomhill, is straighforward: the work is little more than relaying the track and reinstatement of a bridge, over a road, which was taken out by the local authority with agreement to put it back when needed. It is beyond Broomhill that the expensive part comes, notably in providing a new bridge over the River Dulnain, and another over the A95 at Gaich where road improvements, carried out during the interval between closure of the railway and purchase of the trackbed, resulted in demolition of a substantial length of embankment. Nevertheless, sources of finance are being investigated, and it is the aim of the Strathspey Railway Company that it should be back in Grantown before its second decade of passenger services is complete.

## THE  LOCHTY  RAILWAY

*T*he Lochty Railway might well have folded after *Union of South Africa* returned to the tracks of British Rail in 1973. In fact this line, which was established as the first preserved steam railway in Scotland in the peculiar circumstances mentioned in the previous chapter, has survived to become a modest but enduring part of the Scottish railway scene, and uses smaller but perhaps more appropriate locomotives to haul its passenger trains.

Originally, the line of which John B. Cameron was fortunate enough to acquire part was the East Fife Central Railway. This was built by the North British Railway about 1898: it left an existing railway at Leven, filled a gap in the railway map across central Fife and terminated in, apparently, the middle of nowhere at Lochty. There was never, so far as I am aware, a passenger service, but the line seems to have prospered modestly on coal and agricultural produce. Among the locomotives used were J36 class 0-6-0s, of which *Maude* at Bo'ness is a surviving example. It was eventually closed in 1964.

After purchase of the final section of the line across Lochty Farm by J.B. Cameron, the Lochty Private Railway was, as mentioned in the last chapter, inaugurated in 1967 by A4 class 4-6-2 no. 60009 *Union of South Africa* running up and down light engine. No statutory authority was required, for the railway was entirely on private land without public road crossings. The locomotive continued to run up and down every Sunday afternoon that summer; a large shed was built to house her the rest of the time. For the 1968 season a coach was purchased from British Railways: an observation car which had been built in 1937 for the *Coronation* express which was hauled by *Union of South Africa* among other locomotives, and had latterly been used on the West Highland line. Lochty loading bank was modified to serve as passenger platform and, with this coach, the Lochty Private Railway's passenger train service was started. Subsequently a small platform was built at Knightsward, a mile away at the other end of the line, and another coach was obtained. With the assistance of members of Glenrothes Model Railway Club, passenger trains powered by 60009 ran on the Lochty Railway for five seasons from 1968 until 1972.

No. 60009 returned to BR track at the beginning of April 1973. A few days later the road transporter which had taken her away re-appeared bringing Austerity 0-6-0 saddle tank locomotive no. 16. This had been rescued from a scrapyard where it had spent some eighteen months, having been sold as scrap after closure of the coal-carrying Wemyss Private Railway upon which it had previously operated. It was to be used regularly on Lochty passenger trains over the next thirteen years, until 1986 when it was withdrawn for overhaul.

Unlike 60009, however, no. 16 has not been alone at Lochty. Another locomotive had in fact arrived a day earlier: an elegant little 0-4-0 saddle tank, built by Peckett in 1915 for the British Aluminium Co. at Burntisland. When it became redundant it was bought for preservation by Ian Fraser who presented it to the Lochty Private Railway. Two more 0-4-0 saddle tank locomotives, both built by Andrew Barclay, have also reached the Lochty Railway. One, built in 1926, was formerly used at Granton gas works, and was subsequently donated to the Strathspey Railway from which it has been loaned to Lochty since 1981. The other was built in 1952 for the National Coal Board which donated it in 1981.

Two more passenger coaches have been acquired, from British Rail. A stock of goods wagons has also been built up. They are used in maintain-

Lochty Railway 0-4-0 saddle tank locomotive was built by Peckett & Sons of Bristol in 1915 and spent its working life at British Aluminium Co.'s Burntisland Works.

BILL ROBERTON

ing the railway, and some are restored to former 'private owner' colours. A former bitumen tank wagon now carries water for locomotives. The Lochty Railway is maintained and operated by the Fife Railway Preservation Group which has also been instrumental in obtaining rolling stock for it. There are a dozen or so active members. Trains run on summer Sundays between the stations at Lochty and Knightsward.

## *BRECHIN*

*T*he Brechin branch has a long history, and to put the Brechin Railway Preservation Society into context a brief resumé of it is necessary. The ancient country town of Brechin, Angus, was connected early to the railway system. A branch line from Bridge of Dun on the Aberdeen Railway was opened on 1 February 1848, the same date that the adjoining section of main line was opened, though Aberdeen itself was not reached until 1850. The Aberdeen Railway was extending the line which eventually became known as the West Coast Route, from England via Stirling, Perth and Forfar, and was amalgamated, in due course, into the Caledonian Railway. Brechin eventually became the terminus of several other branch lines which converged on it, and acquired suitably handsome station buildings.

With the opening of the bridges over the Forth and the Tay, the East

Coast Route became competitive with the West Coast for traffic from the South to Aberdeen: the North British line from the East Coast joined the Caledonian four miles north of Bridge of Dun at Kinnaber Junction. This became famous during the 'races' of the 1890s when East Coast and West Coast trains to Aberdeen competed to reach it first. In recent times the branch from Bridge of Dun to Brechin eventually lost its passenger trains in 1952, and the other branches to Brechin were closed completely. Main line traffic from the South was concentrated on the East Coast Route, and the line from Perth through Forfar was closed to passengers in 1967 when its trains were diverted through Dundee; between Forfar and Bridge of Dun was closed completely but the branch, as it had become, from Kinnaber Junction to Bridge of Dun and Brechin remained open for freight until it too was closed in 1981.

By that time the Brechin Railway Preservation Society had been formed. A main line connection at Kinnaber Junction was, I understand, no longer acceptable to British Rail, which wished, in the interest of High Speed Trains, to realign the track there to eliminate a sharp curve. That was a legacy of the days when the newly-arrived North British laid a connection into already established Caledonian. But the four-mile line from Bridge of Dun to Brechin was purchased by Angus District Council, with assistance from Tayside Region and the Scottish Tourist Board, and in 1982 Caledonian Railway (Brechin) Ltd was incorporated, to become the operating company of the BRPS, and arranged to lease the railway from the council. The new Caledonian Railway company is limited by guarantee, and a charity; it has offered debentures bearing interest at 5 per cent to help finance the line. It aims to operate the branch as a railway museum, and has applied for a light railway order.

In the meantime the preservation society has been seeking members and volunteer staff. Locomotives and rolling stock have been acquired in preparation for re-opening the line. In 1988 the steam locomotive stock comprised two Austerity 0-6-0 saddle tanks, and two 0-4-0 saddle tanks built by Andrew Barclay. There were also seven diesel locomotives and a 1958-built diesel multiple unit. All were owned by individuals, groups or other organisations rather than the operating company. Rolling stock includes several British Railways mark one coaches, an engineer's saloon and an assortment of goods wagons and vans.

Work has been going ahead on restoring Brechin station buildings, and a large goods shed at that station has proved useful as a workshop for restoring and maintaining locomotives. Steam days with train rides have been held at Brechin station on summer Sundays, and there are Santa specials on Sundays in December. There are hopes that the light railway order will be made in 1989.

Summer Sundays see steam days with train rides at Brechin.     BILL ROBERTON

## THE SCOTTISH INDUSTRIAL RAILWAY CENTRE

*A*yrshire did not have so dense a network of railways, nor was it so heavily industrialised, as much of the central belt of Scotland: but it did have a network of branch lines and industrial railways, intricate and indeed individualistic, which served the collieries of the area. It is at one of these collieries, now closed, that the Scottish Industrial Railway Centre has been set up by the Ayrshire Railway Preservation Group. The group is a voluntary organisation with charitable status: it was formed in 1974 and in 1980 leased the site of Minnivey Colliery, Dalmellington. The colliery is closed but many of its buildings remain.

So does much of its railway track, including the link to Pennyvenie Colliery nearly a mile to the east. This was particularly helpful to the ARPG, as Pennyvenie has road access for low loaders which Minnivey lacks, and so the group was able to bring in locomotives and rolling stock this way. The rail connection west from Minnivey, running for a couple of miles to Waterside where it joined the BR (formerly Glasgow &

South Western) Ayr-Dalmellington branch, had been dismantled in 1978 when Minnivey Colliery closed. This was a disadvantage, for at Waterside lay the extensive remains of the Dalmellington Iron Company's ironworks, closed since 1921 but latterly incorporated into National Coal Board installations which included a coal washery and a loading point for coal brought in by road from an open-cast mine. The line from Waterside to Minnivey and Pennyvenie had originally been part of the iron company's system.

In 1981 the Dalmellington and District Conservation Trust was formed, I understand by three local ladies concerned at the loss of heritage of the area – in Victorian times Dalmellington prospered on iron and coal. A prime target of the conservation trust is the ironworks buildings, which include an 1847 blast engine house. The site also includes a four-road locomotive shed, built by the coal board in the 1950s. British Coal ceased its operations there in the winter of 1986-7 and the way seemed clear for railway group and conservation trust to work together towards reinstatement of the rail link. The ARPG purchased the attractive 1856 station building of the long-closed GSWR Waterside station, with the aid of a grant from Strathclyde Regional Council, and hoped to acquire part of the BR branch line.

At this stage, what might have been for the ARPG a disaster occurred when British Coal found that it would be worth obtaining coal by open-cast mining in the vicinity. This meant that the Ayr-Waterside line, latterly disused but not dismantled, was to be re-opened, with British Coal relaying the line from Waterside to Minnivey so that British Rail coal trains could use it to reach a new open-cast loading point. As I write, late in 1988, the track has been relaid and test trains have run, with full use anticipated for 1989.

However these developments, far from obstructing the aspirations of the railway preservation group, have been to its advantage. British coal has done more than re-lay the track needed for its own purposes: it has reinstated the connection to the ARPG tracks at Minnivey, and the group has hopes of being allowed to operate over the British Coal-owned track to Waterside on Sundays when coal traffic is not passing.

The Ayrshire Railway Preservation Group has assembled an interesting collection of industrial locomotives and rolling stock at Minnivey. By 1988 eight steam locomotives were present. All were built by Andrew Barclay Sons & Co. Ltd of Kilmarnock, the oldest in 1912, the newest in 1955. Four of them spent at least part of their working lives at Waterside. A fireless locomotive – one of the only two surviving in Scotland, the other being in the Museum of Transport, Glasgow – was presented to the ARPG by Shell UK Oil in 1985. It had been in regular use until

Fireless locomotive boarded up against the weather at the Scottish Industrial Railway Centre, Dalmellington, was in regular use by Shell UK Oil until as recently as 1985, and is steamed from time to time at Dalmellington.　　BILL ROBERTON

November of that year: the last steam locomotive in commercial operation in Scotland.

There is also a steam crane built as recently as 1957, several diesel locomotives of both standard and narrow gauges, and various wagons. A Manpower Services Commission scheme helped to improve the site in 1986-7, enabling open days to be held with a locomotive or locomotives in steam. During the summer of 1988 there were eight open days, mostly Sundays but with two Saturdays also. On two days the fireless locomotive was demonstrated in operation.

*

In this chapter, four locations have been described which are devoted principally to preservation and operation of steam locomotives and trains. Two more locations where steam locomotive preservation is part of a broader canvas – Prestongrange and Summerlee – are mentioned in chapter eleven.

# MINIATURE AND
# NARROW
# GAUGE
# RAILWAYS

## KERR'S MINIATURE RAILWAY

*B*ack in 1935, Matthew Kerr built a miniature railway at Arbroath, by the sea in West Links Park. Since then, it has carried over one and half million passengers. Not all of them have been carried by steam-hauled trains, but a great many have. Matthew Kerr senior eventually retired in 1978, to be succeeded by his son, Matthew B. Kerr.

Matthew B. Kerr had known the railway all his life – an early postcard shows him as a toddler alongside a line-up of its locomotives. Grown up, he became a school teacher, as he still is, and in 1978 found himself, as he puts it, 'custodian of an institution'. Passengers return again and again, and four generations of the same family have been known to travel in the same coach. Matthew B. Kerr is now sole proprietor of the railway, and operates it on a voluntary, part-time basis with a willing group of friends: profits from fares are all ploughed back.

They have been needed, for in 1978 the railway was starting to show its age, and during the following nine years some £36,000 was put into it in improvements and deferred maintenance – much of the track, for instance, was re-laid for the first time since the 1930s, and station buildings too had to be rebuilt. This railway is indeed a children's seaside ride: but it would be wrong to say it was no more than that, for it is also a miniature railway in which particular attention is paid to following full-size practice. Here are authentic miniature semaphore signals, sprung buffers and three-link couplings, immaculately ballasted track, signal box and footbridge which if not to precise scale are in proportion, and a multi-track terminus.

This attention to reproduction of the overall railway scene was a noteworthy feature of the line even when first built – maybe the pres-

*Firefly* rests on the turntable after day's work on Kerr's Miniature Railway, Arbroath.

ence of the full size East Coast Main Line was an influence, for the minia-ture railway is laid out alongside it. It was first laid to $7\frac{1}{4}$ in. gauge, but proved so popular that reconstruction on the $10\frac{1}{4}$ in. gauge was neces-sary within three years. This meant that carriages could be wide enough for two children, or even a child and an adult, to sit side by side.

Originally the locomotives were steam, several of them built by the noted miniature-locomotive builder H. C. S. Bullock of Farnborough. But in due course internal combustion locomotives were added, and eventually the last steam locomotive was sold in the early 1960s and for twenty five years or so the line was operated by internal combustion. Some of the i.c. locomotives were 'pretend engines', steam outline pow-ered by an i.c. engine, and one of these, which remains on the line, has with the passage of time become an item of interest in its own right. *Auld Reekie* is a 4-4-2 of North British Railway outline (the full-size version ran on the adjoining main line, but has long since disappeared), built in 1936 and powered by a 1924 Austin Seven petrol engine concealed in the tender. Vintage car enthusiasts arrive from time to time to admire it.

However interesting they may be, such imitation steam locomotives are no substitute for the real thing. To re-introduce steam traction became one of Matthew B. Kerr's ambitions, and was met to a limited extent by the loan from Michael Oliver (to whom reference is made later in this chapter) of his 4-6-0 based on an LMS Class Five. Perhaps this only whetted the appetite; at any rate M. B. Kerr was eventually able to locate, and purchase, a steam locomotive remarkably appropriate for his line. This is the 0-6-0 no. 3007 *Firefly,* built by H. C. S. Bullock in 1936.

Originally a pannier tank locomotive, she had been rebuilt long before with a tender, and has inside Walschaerts valve gear, an unusual arrangement. She has an impressive history, and at one time belonged to Captain J. E. P. Howey, chairman and in effect proprietor of the 15 in. gauge Romney Hythe & Dymchurch Railway – she was the first locomotive to operate there, on a mile of track temporarily re-gauged, when the RH & DR was de-requisitioned from wartime service in 1945. Subsequently she ran for many years on the miniature railway along the foreshore at Hastings, and was twice re-boilered.

Nowadays at Arbroath *Firefly* usually operates on Summer Saturdays (though there were thoughts of altering this to Sundays, or indeed running her on both days). Internal combustion locomotives still power most trains, and Kerr's Miniature Railway is open at weekends from Easter until the end of September, and every day during school summer holidays, that is during July and the first half of August.

## THE MULL RAILWAY

*D*espite the proposals of Lord Leverhulme and others, no passenger-carrying railway ever ran in the Hebrides. Until, that is, 1983, when the Mull & West Highland Narrow Gauge Railway started operations on Mull between Craignure and Torosay. It is not a very big railway – just over one mile long and $10\frac{1}{4}$ in. gauge – but in much, though not all, of its equipment it exemplifies a recent trend to regard such lines as narrow gauge rather than miniature railways, that is to say locomotives and rolling stock are built as large as possible for the gauge, to accommodate full-size staff and passengers, rather than being made as scale miniatures of full-size railway equipment.

The incentive to build the line came from the decision taken in 1975 to open Torosay Castle (in fact, a handsome early Victorian country house) and its gardens to the public. Torosay Castle is a long mile-and-a-half from the ferry terminal at Craignure by a road which though pleasant is unspectacular – just far enough, that is, to discourage day visitors from Oban from heading for it on foot. But the original owner of Torosay had started to build a drive from the castle to the old pier at Craignure, only to find that, when he reached his march, permission to continue across the kirk glebe beyond was unforthcoming. Over a century later the unused drive beneath the rhododendrons had the potential to become the trackbed for a railway, which could then be extended along

Miniature or narrow gauge? Mull railway train passes through the grounds of Torosay Castle.

MULL & WEST HIGHLAND N.G. RAILWAY

the shoreline to Craignure by a route which did offer spectacular views up Loch Linnhe.

The Mull & West Highland Narrow Gauge Railway Co. Ltd. was incorporated in 1976, its primary object being, in the usual all-embracing phraseology of such things, 'To purchase or otherwise acquire, take upon lease, use, construct, equip, operate and work for the conveyance of passengers, goods, livestock and all kinds of merchandise the railway line between Craignure and Torosay Castle, Isle of Mull, and any other railway line.' Directors included the late David James, owner of Torosay, and surveyor and island resident Graham Ellis who has already been mentioned in connection with locomotive 44871. P. A. Ross, the present chairman, became a director in 1981. Because the projected railway lay entirely on Torosay estate, and crossed no public road, no light railway order or other statutory authority was needed.

Before the company was formed, planning permission had been obtained – sadly not without opposition by a neighbouring owner. This was to be but one of the ways in which the promoters of the little railway found that they were re-encountering many of the problems which had faced builders of big railways a century or so before. The route, for instance, apparently so straightforward, produced problems. It involved crossing a bog, where a modern fabric material was used in place of the brushwood foundation upon which earlier builders constructed railways across Chat Moss and Rannoch Moor. A rock cutting had to be blasted at the summit of the line, to keep it to an acceptable level: even so, there is a length of 1 in 52 on the approach to the Mull Railway's own 'Beattock'.

Meanwhile a supporters' organization, the Friends of the Mull Railway, had been formed. Some of the construction work was done by voluntary labour. The Friends made a useful contribution to financing the line too, but most finance was raised by issue of shares in the railway company. Many of them were issued to directors, and the Highlands & Islands Development Board subscribed for £22,000-worth in 1983 and now has a controlling interest. There was also a grant from the HIDB of £30,000 and a loan of £10,000; other loans were made by directors.

Building even a small railway is a big job. The Mull railway needed 23 tonnes of rail, 3,000 sleepers (cut from locally grown timber), 1,500 tonnes of ballast. It was late August 1983 before an experimental passenger train service started. The full service started the following Easter, and the railway was formally declared open on 22 June 1984 by Chris Green, then general manager of ScotRail, and Mrs Green.

Pride and joy of the Mull railway's motive power is the steam locomotive *Lady of the Isles*. This 2-6-4 tank locomotive was built in 1981 by Roger Marsh Ltd and loaned to a miniature railway in Suffolk for two seasons before she came to Mull. A miniature-outline 4-4-2 *Waverley*, originally built by David Curwen in 1948, was being re-boilered during 1988. There are several internal combustion locomotives including the diesel hydraulic *Glen Auldyn* which was built on Mull. Rolling stock includes eight bogie coaches and three ballast wagons. It is anticipated that more coaches will be provided.

There are stations at Craignure (Old Pier), where a new station building has been erected in traditional style, and at Torosay, where the locomotive shed is situated. Maintenance has been hampered by lack of mains electricity, though in 1988 this was expected soon to come to Torosay. Much of the maintenance has been undertaken under contract by engineer Bob Davies of Aros.

A passing loop part-way along the line bears the unlikely name of Tarmstedt. It was near the village of this name in north Germany that David James, during the 1940s, was held as prisoner-of-war. A narrow gauge steam train, which even then seemed archaic, from Bremen to Tarmstedt formed the last stage in the journey into captivity – and the first stage on the journey out of it, for James escaped twice, and the second time was successful in reaching home. His adventures were entertainingly described in his book *A Prisoner's Progress*, which is still available at Torosay, or was until recently.

By curious coincidence, the present author must have been one of the few other people to have known both Torosay and Tarmstedt long before anyone thought of building the Mull railway. In 1950 I took part in a family holiday at Torosay Castle which was then being operated as a hotel – Mull, despite its other attractions seemed regrettably rail-less, though the journeys to and fro, in the sleeping cars which then traversed the Callander & Oban line, remain memorable. Five years later, as a national serviceman stationed in north Germany, I was retaining some approach to normality by exploring, on the few days off, the narrow gauge light railways which still operated there. The metre gauge Kleinbahn Bremen-Tarmstedt, I found, had fallen on hard times. The Bremen end of it was closed, and I had to take successively a tram and then a bus to reach Falkenberg on the outskirts. Thence a railcar, with an older steam train coach as trailer, carried me to Tarmstedt, where steam locomotives could still be glimpsed through the windows of the shed. The next issue of the timetable announced that from November 1955 the service would be entirely by bus. I had, I think, at that date quite forgotten James's book, and it was some years before I re-read it and realised that other British people had travelled the Tarmstedt line before me, in very different circumstances.

To return to Mull: the Mull railway pattern of operation is to run at Easter, then from the end of April to the beginning of October. Trains connect with CalMac ferries arriving from Oban; not all are steam-hauled. Traffic varies: Monday 28 July 1988 produced the worst July storms for fifty years and a mere two intrepid passengers all day. Two days later the railway's resources were stretched to carry nearly 500. Such are the problems of running a tourist railway in the Hebridean climate! Overall, as mentioned in chapter one, 1988 traffic was good. The railway has operated at a profit since 1985, profits which are ploughed back.

*I*n *The Railways of Scotland* (1890)
W. M. Acworth, that informed and entertaining commentator upon the
railway scene, remarked that whereas the Highland Railway was all
main line, the Great North of Scotland was all branches. His point was
that although their route mileages were comparable at 415 and 316
miles respectively, the Highland Railway straggled through the infertile
Highlands from Perth to Wick, but the Great North concentrated a
much denser network into a smaller area, the prosperous agricultural
North East. Unfortunately agriculture was later one of the first industries to turn away from rail to road, with the consequence that today
most of the Highland system remains open, however unpromising the
terrain, but the Great North, apart from its most important line from
Aberdeen to Keith, is almost entirely closed.

After all that it will come as no surprise to learn that it is at the terminus of one of those closed branches that one can in the late 1980s find a
steam locomotive in action. The terminus is Alford, the locomotive *Saccharine*, and the railway upon which it runs is the Alford Valley Railway.

The Alford Valley Railway Co. Ltd was formed in 1979 to construct
and operate a 2 ft gauge passenger railway from Alford railway station to
Bridge of Alford. The attraction of the route was to link Haughton Country Park and caravan and camping site, a mile or so to the north
of Alford, with the Grampian Transport Museum. This museum is
mentioned in chapter eleven, and was then in process of becoming
established. Railway and museum have, however, remained separate
entities which work together.

It is only at the GNSR station itself that the new railway occupies the
trackbed of the old. It leaves – by a very sharp curve – from what was
formerly the terminus end of the station, and heads across country on a
new route. It is operated in two sections, mostly by diesel power; the
steam locomotive appears perhaps a dozen times a year on the occasion
of the main events at the transport museum.

Locomotive *Saccharine* was built by Fowler of Leeds in 1914 and
worked in a South African sugar cane plantation. One feels there should
be a story somewhere in how a sugar plantation steam locomotive came
to be named after a sugar substitute, and, what is more, one derived
from coal: but whatever the origin of the name may be, it seems now to
be forgotten. The locomotive came to Alford in 1979, a free gift which
cost £3,500 to transport. She is a 0-4-2 tank, large for the gauge, weighing some fourteen tons in working order. Like the locomotives of the

GNSR before her, her style of cab reflects the climate in which she worked: but whereas their cabs were closed in against the cold, *Saccharine's* cab, intended for a hot climate, comprises no more than a roof mounted on uprights. On her left-hand tank is mounted a turbo-generator to power electric lights, something to which few locomotives intended to work in Britain aspired. The author confesses to a partiality for locomotives of this size and gauge: they have never been common in Scotland, and it was pleasant to trundle up and down on the footplate of *Saccharine* on a sunny June day. The coach to which she was attached had the body of an 1895 Aberdeen electric tramcar, recovered from summer-house condition.

The former carriage shed of the GNSR at Alford station has had 2 ft gauge track laid into it, and has become the new railway's works. Trains leave from the platform of the old station; the station building houses the Alford Valley Railway Museum, which is part of the Grampian Transport Museum and so is mentioned below, and the local tourist information office.

## LINES PROPOSED FOR STEAM

*T*wo groups which may in due course operate steam trains were making progress during 1988. The Lowthers Railway Society Ltd was laying 2 ft gauge track between Leadhills and Wanlockhead, high in the Southern Uplands, on the course of the former standard gauge light railway which served those villages. The society originated in 1983, and re-formed as a guarantee company in 1986. In 1988 all its motive power was internal combustion: there were hopes of acquiring a steam locomotive or locomotives in due course, depending on availability and finance.

By contrast the embryonic Lochgilphead Miniature Railway has two steam locomotives but no permanent track. The railway is proposed by Bryan Passey and Mike Oliver, who is also closely associated with the Mull railway. The two locomotives are both 10¼ in. gauge. One is a miniature of an LMS class five, built in 1950 and numbered 5156 *Ayrshire Yeomanry*; largely rebuilt, she has as mentioned run on loan on Kerr's Miniature Railway. The other is a miniature of LNER no. 4472 *Flying Scotsman*, built in 1949 but almost totally rebuilt at Lochgilphead between 1981 and 1986.

These locomotives are operated with coaches on temporary track at

Miniature *Flying Scotsman*, one of the locomotives for the proposed Lochgilphead Miniature Railway, runs on temporary track at Lochgilphead in 1986.

fêtes and similar functions; such operations included a three-day stint at the Scottish Exhibition Centre in February 1988. In this way money is being raised towards construction of a permanent line. Application has been made to the Highlands & Islands Development Board for financial assistance, and formation of a company is being considered.

### SEVEN AND A QUARTER INCHES GAUGE

*I*t is not my intention here to provide a full survey of miniature railways in Scotland, but two further lines do deserve mention. Both are built to $7\frac{1}{4}$ in. gauge, and operate steam trains. Strathaven Miniature Railway dates back some forty years, for it was first laid in 1949. Its continued operation today is a joint effort by East Kilbride District Council and Strathaven Model Society ('Model Society' because running the miniature railway is but one of its activities, which also include model boats and model aircraft). The district council provides the site, in George Allan Park, Strathaven, Lanarkshire, and in the early 1980s provided the materials for new track to replace the old, which was worn out. The new system in fact incorporates not only $7\frac{1}{4}$ in. gauge, but also narrower gauges, both on the ground and raised.

The model society maintains the railway and runs public passenger trains every Saturday and Sunday from Easter until the end of September. The regular locomotive is a fine 2-6-0 of Great Western Railway outline which was built locally in the late forties at the time the line itself was built. Originally gifted to the former Fourth District Council of Lanarkshire County Council, it is now in effect held in trust for the line by the club. It was restored in the mid-seventies after an interval when the line was worked by internal combustion, but by 1988 needed reboilering. It was hoped that the new boiler will be made and fitted for the 1989 season. Other locomotives which belong to club members operate on the line, and so from time to time do those of visitors. Notable among the former is a $7\frac{1}{4}$ in. gauge version of a Highland Railway Jones Goods 4-6-0.

The grounds of the House of Ross, Comrie, Perthshire, are hilly and wooded, a rewarding location for the $7\frac{1}{4}$ in. gauge railway which is under construction there. It is privately owned and on private ground, but it is usually opened to the public at least one day a year – at the time of 'Comrie Fortnight' in late July – and may be open more often in future. The first section, forming a circuit round a small hill, was built with aluminium rails by Professor P. M. B. Walker, former owner of the House of Ross who is still resident nearby; a much longer circuit of steel rail is being added by retired marine engineer Bob Smith.

Engineering works on the new section which have been completed so far include several rock cuttings and embankments, two level crossings over a private road, three viaducts of which one is a timber trestle and another, the largest, has spans made from crane jib sections, and a longish hillside shelf beside a lochan among the oakwoods. Curves are frequent and gradients steep, which leads to spirited performance by the locomotives. Resident locomotives (visitors appear from time to time) are all miniatures of narrow gauge locomotives. Two are free-lance: a 2-4-0 tank and tender locomotive *Auld Reekie*, and a 0-4-2 tank and tender locomotive of American outline inspired by the locomotives of Hawaiian sugar cane plantations; and two are derived from full-size prototypes, respectively a 0-4-2 tank locomotive modelled on the Talyllyn Railway's no. 1, and a magnificent 2-8-2 modelled on the 3 ft gauge 2-8-2s of the Denver & Rio Grande Western Railroad in Colorado.

# $L$ O C H
# $S$ T E A M E R S

## *L O C H   K A T R I N E   A N D* S I R   W A L T E R   S C O T T

$T$he Loch Katrine steamer *Sir Walter Scott* has a most remarkable record of service. She (for even with so masculine a name, a ship cannot be anything but she) was launched on to the loch in 1899; and in the late 1980s, without hint of preservation or preservation society, she continues to carry tourists upon Loch Katrine. During that long period since her launch, the turbine steamer on the Clyde has come and gone, and the steam locomotive, once present in enormous numbers, has in effect disappeared from the railway system; but the Loch Katrine steamer continues to ply just as she has always done. When she was new, passenger steamers on inland lochs and lakes were common, and on the coast they were commoner. Their eventual decline has meant that *Sir Walter Scott* has become unique – she is the only surviving screw steamship in Scotland carrying passengers to a regular schedule. Furthermore she burns solid fuel – coal until 1967, smokeless fuel subsequently – and her furnaces are stoked by hand.

The reason behind her survival in this form is that the loch is used to supply Glasgow with drinking water, as it has been since 1859, and no risk of contamination by oil is permissible. Nor is there a public road for motor vehicles along the loch shore: a private road which follows it is available to the public only on foot or bicycle. Otherwise, to enjoy the scenery of Loch Katrine, one must go on the steamer – and the scenery has been famous since Sir Walter Scott himself made it so at the beginning of the last century. The first steamer put on the loch, in 1843, is said to have been scuttled by the crew of a rowing galley accustomed to tak-

SS *Sir Walter Scott* approaches Trossachs Pier, Loch Katrine, in September 1988.

AUTHOR

ing tourists in their own vessel. She was soon replaced, however, and in due course superseded by a third steamer which lasted until soon after *Sir Walter Scott* arrived.

Although *Sir Walter Scott* is now old, she is by no means primitive. On the contrary, by 1899, the date she was ordered, steamship design was long past the formative stage, and was well established. In this respect she makes an interesting comparison with her contemporary, the Royal Museum of Scotland's 1900 Locomobile steam car, from which it is clear that car manufacturers then still had a lot to learn. But by that date shipbuilders knew very well how to design and build an elegant and comfortable excursion steamer such as *Sir Walter Scott*, and her appearance and level of passenger comfort, to which the quiet and largely vibration-free steam engine makes a big contribution, remain entirely acceptable to this day. More-recent developments in shipbuilding, one feels, have been for the most part only in the direction of economy of construction and operation.

Builder William Denny & Bros. of Dumbarton made *Sir Walter Scott* 110 ft long by 19 ft beam, with a triple expansion engine and two boilers by M. Paul & Co., Dumbarton, from whom, curiously, the ship herself was a sub-contract. The ship was ordered by the Loch Katrine Steamboat Co. Ltd., and when complete was knocked down, so that the parts could be taken up Loch Lomond by barge to Inversnaid, and then overland to Stronachlachar near the western end of Loch Katrine, where she was re-erected and launched.

Her immediate predecessor SS *Rob Roy* was held in reserve until 1908 and then scrapped: subsequently *Sir Walter Scott* alone has carried tourists up and down the loch between Trossachs Pier and Stronachlachar. Eventually she was taken over from the steamboat company by Glasgow Corporation, which wished to have full control over its water supply, so ownership today has descended to the Water Department of Strathclyde Regional Council which operates the ship. (Connoisseurs of bureaucratic anomalies may, however, like to note that the whole of Loch Katrine, and its steamer, lie physically well within Central Region.)

As built, *Sir Walter Scott* had neither wheelhouse nor awnings over the deck: both features are later additions. She is however still propelled by her original engine, which can be seen from the deck through the engine-room skylights. Her original boilers were replaced in 1956 by two new ones, each with a single furnace, built by Marshall & Anderson Ltd. of Motherwell. These in their turn are now getting old, so it was good to learn in 1988 from Mr F. R. Khan, Water Department Area Engineer, that at their last survey it was noted that despite their age the boilers appear to be in good condition, and perhaps could last for another ten years or so. The ship is operated by a crew of six: captain, mate, engineer, stoker and two deckhands. Captain and engineer do maintenance work on her in winter, while the rest of the crew are assigned to other work in the locality.

*Sir Walter Scott*'s route is neither long nor laborious, for Trossachs Pier and Stronachlachar are no more than 7 miles and 45 minutes steaming apart. Perhaps this has contributed to her longevity. Formerly, round tours from Edinburgh and Glasgow were offered by road, rail and ship, incorporating both the Loch Katrine steamer and the Loch Lomond steamer between Inversnaid and Balloch: but these were discontinued when PS *Maid of the Loch* was taken out of service on Loch Lomond, as mentioned below. *Sir Walter Scott* does, however, receive much useful traffic from coach tour operators, and it is largely to suit them that she now makes two out-and-back hour-long cruises from Trossachs Pier every summer afternoon, and travels up to Stronachlachar and back in the mornings, Monday to Friday inclusive. The season lasts from the beginning of May until the end of September.

*Sir Walter Scott*'s career though long has been simple: there is neither complexity nor controversy to describe. A recent visit by the author found her, although it was towards the end of the season, immaculate in gleaming white and red paint and polished brass. Hopefully it will be possible for a long time to come to follow that most unlikely of approaches, the narrow undulating winding road far inland through the Trossachs woods and hills, to find at the end of it a pier with a real steamer ready to depart.

## LOCH AWE AND LADY ROWENA

*T*hroughout Britain there is no other stretch of water from which, until recently, the absence of steamers or passenger vessels was more conspicuous than Loch Awe. Loch Awe is twenty three miles or so long, the longest of all British inland lochs or lakes. By the early years of this century, steamers plied its length from Ford at the south to Loch Awe station pier at the north, and formed a link in a through route from Glasgow to Oban which brought tourists by Clyde steamer to Ardrishaig and thence by coach to Ford; and subsequently took them from Loch Awe to their destination by train. Other short distance steamers connected the station with lochside hotels such as Portsonachan, cargo steamers carried goods and timber up and down the loch, and the big houses along the shores of the loch ran their own steam launches. Even in the late 1930s when the LMS Railway built three motor vessels to carry passengers on inland waters, two were for Windermere and the third, the *Countess of Breadalbane*, for Loch Awe.

After a gap during the Second World War, however, it proved impossible to revive the service in the unprosperous times which followed, and after four seasons the ship was removed from the loch in 1952 and taken overland to the Clyde: eventually, as mentioned below, she became *Countess Fiona* on Loch Lomond. By the late 1960s, when the author first knew the district, Loch Awe station was closed and the loch itself, which had previously seen so much activity, appeared to support no vessels larger than anglers' dinghies. Nor did there seem any prospect of change.

In the altered climate of the mid-eighties, however, there were two developments. One was that Loch Awe station was re-opened in 1985, by British Rail in conjunction with The Holiday Fellowship Ltd. Holiday Fellowship was by then operating the Victorian Scottish Baronial building of the Loch Awe Hotel, on its crag above the station, as a guest house called Loch Awe House.

The other development at the same period was that Harry Watson, Glasgow surgical instrument manufacturer with experience of steam engines and a desire to own a boat, knew of the 'vacancy' on Loch Awe. In 1984 he had obtained the hull of a 36 ft Windermere launch built in 1926, and early in 1985 set up the Dalriada Steam Packet Co. Ltd with himself and wife Averil as principal shareholders. The hull was restored and fitted with new steam plant, a vertical firetube boiler and a compound engine (cylinder sizes $3\frac{3}{4}$ in. and 6 in. diameter by $4\frac{1}{2}$ in. stroke) both built by Langley Engineering of Storrington, Sussex. Peat, eventually, was found to be entirely adequate as fuel.

The old steamer pier at Loch Awe station was done up by British Rail and leased to the company. The boat was passed by the Department of Trade to carry thirty passengers, and named *Lady Rowena* after the heroine of Scott's *Ivanhoe*, perpetuating a long-standing Scottish tradition of steamer names connected with that author and his works. All this took very much longer to achieve than to tell. It was July 1986 before the boat was first steamed, public cruises were started, and devotees began to make their way to Loch Awe to experience steam revived after an interval of fifty years or so.

And not, fortunately, just devotees. The Highlands & Islands Development Board has helped with publicity (and also with finance). The first full season, 1987, saw about 3,000 passengers. Sailings con-

SL *Lady Rowena* lands passengers at Dalavich, Loch Awe. AUTHOR

nected with trains at the re-opened station, and Loch Awe station pier is also easy of access by the A85 road. At first the cruises were in effect tours of the north-eastern end of the loch lasting three-quarters of an hour or so, but later in the season *Lady Rowena* was being taken down the loch to Dalavich to offer cruises thence one day a week, and for 1988 a much wider range of cruises was offered with visits also, according to the day of the week, to Ardanaseig's noted gardens, and Portsonachan Hotel.

In 1988 also, to provide a waiting and refreshment room for *Lady Rowena*'s passengers at Loch Awe station pier, a railway coach was obtained from British Rail which delivered it to an isolated length of track by slewing the main line over and then reinstating it. The actual coach was formerly in use on the Fort William-Mallaig steam train.

Because of the complexity of operation, and the skills which need to be developed, running a small steam plant has a fascination that running an internal combustion engine lacks. That same characteristic becomes a disadvantage as soon as it is intended to operate any sort of regular service – hence the numerous 'pretend engines' of miniature railways. To operate a scheduled service with a steam launch is a brave endeavour anywhere: it is doubly so when the service is set up in an area remote from centres of population, where the marine and steam engineering facilities and skills needed for technical backup are alike absent. Those who wish to help can now join The Friends of *Lady Rowena:* the address for enquiries about *Lady Rowena* and her friends is on page 140.

## LOCH LOMOND AND THE MAID

*T*he steamer services on Loch Lomond were in many ways a lesser version of those on the Clyde. Paddle steamers came early to the loch - the first, the *Marion*, started to ply there in 1817. The first railway in the district, opened in 1850, ran from Bowling on the Clyde to Balloch pier at the foot of Loch Lomond, linking the steamer services of the two waterways, and was only later connected with the expanding railway system. Subsequently the Loch Lomond steamers came into railway ownership and, as on the Clyde, the services they provided became part of a combined rail/water route, in this case between Glasgow and the places served by piers up the loch. People travelled on them for business, and, particularly on so famous and beautiful a stretch of water, they cruised for pleasure.

By the early 1950s the two paddle steamers remaining on the loch, dating from 1911 and 1898, were becoming elderly, and British Railways ordered a new one: this, *Maid of the Loch,* was, like *Waverley,* built by A & J Inglis and engined by Rankin & Blackmore; she was built at Pointhouse, knocked down and taken in parts to Balloch, and there re-assembled, with oil-burning three-furnace boiler and compound engine. She entered service in May 1953, the last paddle steamer built for British waters. She was also very, very large for the service she was to operate – 191 ft long and with a certificate for 1,000 passengers. Within a couple of years the two older steamers had been withdrawn and *Maid of the Loch* alone provided the service.

By the mid-1960s *Maid of the Loch* was owned by Caledonian Steam Packet Co. Ltd, and was operating at a loss, but additional publicity improved the passenger figures. When Caledonian Steam Packet was transferred from British Rail to the Scottish Transport Group in 1969, *Maid of the Loch* was transferred on paper to Walter Alexander & Sons (Midland) Ltd, an STG bus-operating subsidiary: in practice she was operated and publicised as part of the Caledonian MacBrayne fleet. In this fleet she came to seem increasingly anachronistic as a vessel – after

1977 she was its only surviving steamer – and increasingly out of place in the type of service offered. While other routes were ruthlessly converted to short-distance vehicle ferries, the Loch Lomond steamer continued, with the aid of handsome subsidies from local authorities, to provide a longitudinal service, connecting with trains at Balloch Pier and serving the piers up the loch at Luss (re-opened in 1980 after thirty-one years' closure), Rowardennan, Tarbet and Inversnaid. Because of the lack of a road along the east shore of the loch north of Rowardennan, these places are in most cases much more conveniently linked by water than by land.

Nevertheless after the 1981 season CalMac withdrew *Maid of the Loch* from service, and put her up for sale. Reporting this on 21 January 1982, the *Glasgow Herald* stated that in 1981 the steamer had carried 114,000 passengers, twenty per cent more than 1980: yet after regional and district council subsidies totalling £128,000, there had been a loss of £73,450. (It is not clear whether the passenger figure quoted was for bookings or passenger-journeys, but whichever it may have been the figure is not unimpressive.)

The successful bidder for *Maid of the Loch* was Alloa Brewery Co. Ltd, a subsidiary of the brewing-catering group Allied Lyons plc. Alloa Brewery saw in the ship potential for a static bar and restaurant complex as well as for loch cruising. To establish her as such, however, was dependent on the progress of other loch-shore developments: and although the area around the southern end of Loch Lomond is somewhat run-down, there seems to be such a tangle of ownerships, local authorities, local planning authorities and other groups with opinions about what should or should not be done around the loch, that the effect seems to be that very little is achieved at all.

Alloa Brewery both foresaw that progress with *Maid of the Loch* might be slow, and wished to maintain the service she had been providing. So what it did was what might have been done decades before: it put on a smaller ship. And although *Countess Fiona* is and has always been a motor vessel, she is such a fine little vintage ship, and so appropriate for her task, that to overlook her here would be pedantic to excess. As mentioned previously she was built in 1936 as *Countess of Breadalbane* for the LMS railway's shipping service on Loch Awe. After this was withdrawn in 1951 she was taken overland to the Clyde, where Caledonian Steam Packet used her for some years and then sold her out of service, so that eventually Alloa Brewery was able to purchase her and return her to inland waters on Loch Lomond. Re-named, she entered service there in 1982: and since then has successfully operated between Balloch and the piers up the loch. *Maid of the Loch*, with capacity for 1,000 passen-

Balloch Pier, Loch Lomond, on 25 September 1986: PS *Maid of the Loch* lies out of use, and the pier railway station, for which the overhead wiring can be seen to the right, was closed a few days after this photograph was taken. At least the shipping service to the piers up the loch is still maintained by MV *Countess Fiona*, left.

AUTHOR

gers and a crew of 33 was unable to do so without a large subsidy: *Countess Fiona*, with capacity for 180 passengers and a crew of 6, covers her costs unsubsidised.

In this, she cannot have been helped by closure of the railway line to Balloch Pier station at the end of the 1986 season, when Strathclyde Passenger Transport Executive (controlled by Strathclyde Region) withdrew financial support. Passengers arriving by train to join the ship are now faced by a twenty-minute walk, wet or fine, from Balloch Central which has become the terminus. According to the public notice of closure, savings were estimated to be £5,000 a year to British Rail and £10,000 a year to the PTE. Such sums are minuscule in transport operating terms, and the closure contrasted markedly with re-opening of other railways and stations at the same period – notably Loch Awe station in 1985, as mentioned above.

However, Alloa Brewery Co. Ltd's continuing commitment to Loch Lomond cruising – long-haul cruising, not just 'round-the-bay' operations – is wholly laudable. Its guardianship of *Maid of the Loch* has been less happy. Since 1981, the ship has lain out of use alongside Balloch pier. Passengers for *Countess Fiona* cross her deck to go aboard. Her condition has deteriorated slowly (volunteers from the Paddle Steamer Preservation Society have attempted to protect her from damage likely to be caused by leaking decks) and her boiler is now old and in bad condition and needs replacement before the ship could steam again. But Alloa Brewery Co. feels in any case that for the sort of operation which it would prefer, that is to say a static restaurant for perhaps six days a week and a cruising one for the seventh, steam propulsion would be uneconomic. It envisages removal of the steam plant and installation of diesel power to drive the paddle wheels. Economically speaking, that is no doubt quite correct. But one of the great attractions of a paddle steamer to passengers – and not just to committed steam buffs – is the open engine room, the impressive sight of the rods and cranks of a very large steam engine at work. Removal of *Maid of the Loch*'s steam plant would remove an important attraction for visitors. It would certainly be much regretted by a great many people, for real paddle steamers do not come two-a-penny in the late 1980s. Another option which has been considered would be establishment of a trust to preserve the ship as a Loch Lomond information centre: a static one. At the time of writing (October 1988) the future of *Maid of the Loch* remains undecided.

Since the above was written, the *Daily Telegraph* (3 May 1989) has reported that PS *Maid of the Loch* has been bought by partners Stuart Ballantyne and James Fisher and Sons, who intend to restore her.

# $S$*HIPS* $A$*ND*
# $T$*HEIR*
# $E$*NGINES*

$I$f the paddle steamer was the vessel most closely associated with the Clyde, then the Clyde Puffer ran it a very close second. Clyde Puffers or, more properly, steam lighters carried cargo throughout the Clyde, the West Coast and the islands. Early examples exhausted used steam to atmosphere and puffed like locomotives, hence the name, which survived installation of condensers in later vessels. Their dimensions were limited by the locks of the Forth & Clyde Canal, through which they passed and beside which many were built. This meant they were short – 66 feet or so – and relatively beamy, about 18 ft 6 in. But their draught could be as much as 8 ft 6 in., which meant they showed a lot of hull when unladen, and their air draught, on a canal where all the bridges opened for the benefit of sailing ships, was unlimited. The consequence was a ship with a short, stubby upright appearance: and a jaunty character matched by that of the Clyde Puffer's most famous fictional skipper. For disdain mingled with affection in popular regard for the Clyde Puffer, so much so that Neil Munro was able to use one and its crew as the vehicle for his tales of perspicacity and wit that are the Para Handy stories. Para Handy the skipper, MacPhail the engineer, and the rest of the crew of the steam lighter *Vital Spark*, with their mixture of innocence and guile, continue to delight new generations of readers, and of television viewers, long after real steam puffers have ceased to trade.

In 1943 the then Ministry of War Transport adopted the Clyde Puffer design for a series of 54 victualling inshore craft (VICs) for the Royal Navy, to supply stores, ammunition and water to the fleet. Why it perpetuated such restricted dimensions, when even puffer owners had been building longer ships for West Coast use between the wars, is a minor mystery. One is tempted to speculate whether even at that late date the powers-that-be thought the ability to pass by canal between naval installations on the Clyde and those on the Forth would be advantageous. At any rate it is to construction of this late batch of puffers that we owe survival of two in working order in Scotland at the present day. They are *Auld Reekie,* formerly *VIC 27,* and *VIC 32.* Both were built in 1943, respectively by I. Pimblott & Co. of Northwich, Cheshire and R. Dunston & Co. of Thorne, Yorkshire – nearly all these wartime puffers were built south of the border. Each has a vertical boiler by Cochran & Co. of Annan and a two-cylinder compound engine by Crabtree & Co. of Great Yarmouth.

*VIC 27* was laid up about 1962, and eventually purchased in 1968 by Sir James Miller, chairman of James Miller & Partners Ltd, building and civil engineering contractors. He arranged for her hold to be converted into living accommodation, and for her to be chartered out to youth groups, scouts and the like. In this new guise she was re-named *Auld Reekie.* Occasionally she was made available to others, and in the early summer of 1970 the author, his wife and a party of friends made a delectable voyage in her from Oban to Inverness and back, through the Caledonian Canal. Charterers had to help run the ship, for she came with only a skipper and a deckhand (named, implausibly but truly, Tom, and Jerry), and under their patient good-natured guidance we found out much of what it was like to run a small steam coaster, from stoking to steering.

Towards the end of the seventies, *Auld Reekie* was purchased by Bathgate Brothers Marine Ltd, which continued to charter her out. In 1988 she was seen by millions, moored in the harbour area at the Glasgow Garden Festival, masquerading for the occasion as the *Vital Spark.* She had been leased for the duration of the festival by Argyll & Bute District Council, part of whose exhibit she became.

Before attending the festival, *Auld Reekie* was renovated by the council as part of a Manpower Services Commission Community Programme. Earlier she had been holed in the Crinan Canal (not, one gets the impression, a difficult thing to achieve), and renovations included repairs to damage to the hull. To gain access internally the accommodation was removed and the hold returned to original condition. Other work included replacing the roof of the wheelhouse, various doors and ladders, and complete re-painting externally and internally.

After the garden festival *Auld Reekie* steamed to Ardrishaig for the winter. She was no longer available for charter, but her owners were

SS *Auld Reekie*, alias *Vital Spark*, was moored at the Glasgow Garden Festival for the summer of 1988. AUTHOR

considering approaches made to them: her future may lie in a maritime museum or heritage park.

## V I C   3 2

*M*acpha-i-l-l' calls Nick Walker down the speaking tube from *VIC 32*'s wheelhouse to the engine room below, when he wishes to attract his engineers' attention. 'They usually answer to that' he says, and then, lest you think that all this Para Handy stuff is going too far, he adds disarmingly: 'I think it's the bit about the ale that gets them'. Nick and Rachel Walker have been running holiday cruises on *VIC 32* since 1979, with a flair that results in just the right degree of informality and produces an atmosphere of immediate friend-liness.

Back in the mid-1970s, Nick was helping to run a boatyard on the Grand Union Canal at Uxbridge near London: there, he says, he learned what could go wrong with boats. But he hankered after something larger than an English canal boat, and it was while returning from an

abortive visit to Tyneside to inspect one that he called at Whitby and observed a vessel which, though out of place, he found instantly recognisable. He had regularly spent summer holidays at his grandfather's house at Tayvallich, Argyll, not far from the Crinan Canal, in the days when Clyde Puffers on passage through it were a familiar feature: so even on the far-off Yorkshire coast a puffer was unmistakable.

*VIC 32* had been purchased for preservation, but very little had been done, and when Nick first saw her at Whitby she was, it transpired, for sale. He bought her in 1975, for £1500, knowing very little about steam: but he soon found that if you have an interesting enough vessel, people will come forward to help. This was particularly so when he moved her to St Katherine's Haven, London, where she had several other vintage ships and sailing barges for company. Nick and Rachel lived on board, while the ship was gradually overhauled and the hold converted into living accommodation. But he did not intend her to stay there indefinitely: after a cruise to Dieppe, which was perhaps in retrospect over-ambitious, he moved her by stages during the summer of 1978 up the East Coast and through the Caledonian Canal to Crinan. The voyage was organised on the basis that those who took part shared the costs: it was a trial run for holiday cruises in traditional puffer waters which commenced the following year.

During 1988, from the beginning of May until the end of August, *VIC 32*'s programme offered five-day cruises for up to twelve participants on Loch Fyne and the Clyde, based for the most part on Ardrishaig and with no two successive weeks' cruises identical. In September the programme offered five weeks of six-day cruises on the Caledonian Canal. The ship continues to belong to Nick and Rachel Walker, the cruises are operated by Highland Steamboat Holidays Ltd, which they formed to limit their financial risk.

Cruise participants help to run the ship and are invited to indicate on the booking form if any of the following activities interest them:

'Navigation Crew (i.e. on the Bridge, studying charts, wrestling with the wheel and the Captain's temper);

Engineer/Stoker (i.e. getting dirty, burnt, hot and sweaty);

Deckhand (i.e. getting ropes from boat to quay, casting off, etc.);

Deckchair Hand (i.e. keeping clean and watching all the others getting dirty).'

In fact, *VIC 32* does operate with a crew of five – skipper, chief engineer, mate, cook and assistant cook. The latter two, says the skipper

Ardrishaig disappears in the smoke astern as SS *VIC 32* heads down Loch Fyne.

AUTHOR

tactfully, have the hardest job: a challenge to which they were responding magnificently on the day I happened to be aboard, producing a buffet lunch that was very good indeed.

It was a welcome prelude to an afternoon in the engine room. Here, participants in the cruises can study the particular features of a Clyde Puffer's machinery – control by rods from the wheelhouse above, and an engine with the low pressure valve chest positioned not in line with the cylinder, but to one side, with the valve spindle operated by a rocking arm: an arrangement which reduces the length of the engine by about one foot, and presumably lengthens the cargo space by the same amount, valuable in a vessel of restricted length. Here too they can experience the operation of the steam plant in a small ship – oiling round and warming the engine through by letting it turn over gently while the ship is still moored, then stoking, against a blast of blinding heat every time the furnace door is opened, and adjusting the funnel and ashpit dampers to achieve a bright, thin fire.

Those, at least, were this author's instructions. But I had also been warned that we were heading across Loch Fyne, while the wind was blowing force seven up it. I began to wonder how much the ship would roll. Would it be possible to stand, let alone stoke the furnace? Would we end up out of steam, rolling helplessly in the gale, unable to manoeuvre? Before we moved out of shelter I built the fire up rather more than, perhaps, I should.

Inevitably the engine room proved remarkably stable – I suppose a puffer pivots about a centre of gravity to be found in its boiler. Equally inevitably, we arrived in port blowing off with a great deal too much steam, and to a great deal of extensive and appropriate leg-pulling!


## SCOTTISH MARITIME MUSEUM

*T*he Scottish Maritime Museum was founded in 1983 to preserve, interpret and display Scotland's maritime past. It has acquired an impressive and wide-ranging collection of ships, boats and maritime artefacts which are displayed in various premises near the harbour at Irvine, Ayrshire or, as the case may be, afloat in the harbour. A particularly noticeable gap in the collection at the time of writing is the absence of any vessel driven by steam, although the coaster *Kyles* (1872) and the puffer *Spartan* (1942) were originally steam-driven but were converted to motor during their working lives. It is a gap which the museum hopes to fill.

What the museum does have, almost entirely in store but with plans for display, is an extremely important collection of marine steam engines. Most of them were placed on loan in 1985-86 by Glasgow Museums and Art Galleries. The only item currently on display is the oldest, the original 1812 11½ in. diameter cylinder from the engine of Bell's *Comet*. Bell soon realised his ship was underpowered and attempted to alleviate this by fitting a cylinder of 1 in. larger diameter to the engine. The original survived, and is now displayed in the museum's boat shop.

The principal engines loaned by Glasgow Museums are:

Side lever engine believed to have been built for PS *Comet II* by D. McArthur & Co., 1821;

Side lever engine built for PS *Industry* by Caird of Greenock, 1828 – this engine replaced the ship's original engine of 1814 and powered her until withdrawn in 1862, by which date she was the oldest steamer still operating;

High pressure and low pressure turbines built for SS *King Edward* – the first passenger steamer propelled by turbines – by Parsons Marine Steam Turbine Co., Ltd, 1901;

Compound engine – cylinders 17 in. and 34 in diameter by 24 in. stroke – and three auxiliary engines built for the crane barge *Newshot* by Fleming & Ferguson, Paisley, 1943; this vessel, built for the Ministry of Transport, was later transferred to Clyde Navigation Trust and is still in use, powered by internal combustion, on the East Coast;

Three inches to the foot scale exhibition-standard builder's model of steeple engine for P & O Line PS *Simla,* made by Tod & McGregor, 1853.

The museum's own collection includes the engine from the puffer *Sitka* and the patterns for the turbines of the *Queen Elizabeth II.*

To display the steam engines, and its collection of shipyard machinery which includes two steam hammers, the museum has acquired the very large engine shop which was built in 1872 at Alexander Stephen & Sons' Linthouse Engine Works, Govan. During the winter of 1987-88 this was dismantled and moved to Irvine, with grant aid from the National Heritage Memorial Fund. It is intended that, when re-erected, hopefully in the early 1990s, it will become the museum's main exhibition hall. There are also hopes, currently of the crystal-gazing kind, that it may eventually be possible to operate some of the engines under steam. The museum has acquired a compound horizontal steam engine from an Irvine saw mill, which would then be used to drive shipyard machinery by line shafting. In the meantime it may be possible to arrange access to the marine engines by appointment.

The Scottish Maritime Museum was formed as a joint venture by the

West of Scotland Boat Museum Association and Irvine Development Corporation, which set up Scottish Maritime Museum Trust (Irvine) as a company limited by guarantee. Representatives of other bodies such as the district council and academic institutions have been invited to join in running the trust, and the boat museum association, renamed the Scottish Maritime Heritage Association, contributes voluntary labour and functions as its 'Friends of' organization.


OCEAN MIST

*T*he steam yacht *Ocean Mist* was built in 1919; her hull is 125 ft 6 in. long by 23 ft 6 in. beam, and her triple-expansion engine has cylinders of $12\frac{1}{2}$ in, 21 in, and 35 in diameter by 26 in. stroke. She passed through several ownerships; for many years she was based at a mooring at the head of Banavie Locks on the Caledonian Canal, becoming a familiar part of the landscape – so familiar that she appeared in innumerable picture postcards, photographers finding her a convenient feature for the foreground of their pictures of Ben Nevis.

In the mid-1980s she changed hands again and, her steam plant being in good condition, made the voyage under her own steam to Leith. She is now owned by the Leith Steamship Company Ltd and, moored in Leith Harbour, has been converted into a restaurant. S.Y. *Ocean Mist* restaurant opened in August 1988, specialising in – what else – sea food, served from midday, seven days a week, all year, in comfortable surroundings decorated with pictures of famous steam yachts of the past.

*Ocean Mist* is now separated from the sea by a swing bridge which, I understand, no longer swings, and is attached to the shore by connections for mains services. So sadly there is little prospect of her moving. But her owners are aware how interesting her engine room is, for it is complete apart from the fuel tanks which have been removed, and once tidied up they intend to make it accessible for public viewing. Furthermore they are contemplating disconnecting the propeller, firing the boiler by gas, and running that triple-expansion engine under steam. That sounds as if it will be a sight worth seeing.

$\mathcal{T}$he Renfrew-Yoker ferry across
the Clyde is believed to have been the last chain-operated ferry in
Europe when it was replaced by independently-operated boats in 1984.
One of its steam-driven chain-operated vessels survives in the care of
Renfrew District Council, which hopes to open it to the public as a
museum of maritime life; it has already been seen and visited by a great
many of the public during 1988, when it formed the council's contribution to the Glasgow Garden Festival.

There have been ferries across the Clyde for centuries, and for at least
two hundred years prior to 1984 they were pulled across the river using
a fixed rope or chain. Originally they were pulled across manually, by
pulling on the rope; later the rope was passed over a pulley connected to
a larger wheel: turning this made the pulley revolve and moved the ferry
along the rope. In due course steam power was adopted to turn the
wheel, and the rope replaced by a chain or chains, and in the ferry's final
form diesel power was used. The vessel now preserved by Renfrew District Council was built in 1935 by Fleming & Ferguson of Paisley to take
250 passengers and 18 vehicles. When a diesel vessel came into use at
the Renfrew ferry in the late 1960s, she was moved to Erskine ferry, after
first being widened and re-boilered. The Erskine bridge was opened in
1971 and she returned to Renfrew as standby vessel. She remained as
such until 1984, when she was purchased from Clyde Port Authority by
Renfrew District Council.

Subsequent reconditioning and conversion was done partly as an
MSC Community Programme, partly by local firms. She was drydocked
at Greenock for the hull to have its thickness checked, followed by
cleaning and painting. The deck was roofed over to provide display
space. After closure of the garden festival the ferry was towed back to
Renfrew. It is hoped to moor her there permanently and open her to the
public. The two boilers were the only part of the ferry that the district
council was unable to restore during its refurbishment programme, nor
is it likely that finance will be available for restoration. The engine is in
working order and could run under steam if it were available: as a short
term measure an electric motor is provided to turn the engine and the
drive wheel.

CHAPTER TEN

# REPLICA SHIPS
# AND
# BOATS

## THE COMET

$A$s you drive west from Glasgow, the motorway eventually runs out into ordinary dual carriageway, and then the road skirts the town of Port Glasgow, taking a long curve to the left round a large car park, with a high wall on the right. In the unlikely surroundings of the car park you catch a momentary glimpse, out of the corner of your eye, of the full-size replica of Henry Bell's pioneer steam boat *Comet* – momentary, because of course you are keeping your eyes on the road, and for the same reason you totally miss a plaque attached to the wall on the right. What you should then do is turn left into the car park and stop to examine both vessel and plaque.

The latter provides the clue to the former. 'Near this place', it announces, 'the steamship "Comet" was built by John Wood, Ship-builder, Port-Glasgow. Launched on 24th July 1812'. The replica was built 150 years later, in 1962; and though she now stands on concrete plinths in a shallow pond surrounded by vandal-deterrent chain link fencing, she had when built her own moment of glory. For this replica was built as a fully working replica, as accurately as possible, and her launch with steam up on to the Clyde from the same spot as the original was the high point in a week-long programme of 150th anniversary celebrations.

Firm planning for the event had commenced only in March 1962, the leading light being Provost Walter P Lucas, who had taken part in extensive celebrations which marked the centenary of the *Comet* in 1912. Exhibitions and parades were planned, but a centrepiece connected with the original vessel was needed. A statue? A monument? A model?

Engine is lowered into replica *Comet* at Lithgows Ltd's yard, Port Glasgow, in August 1962. NORMAN BURNISTON PHOTOGRAPHY

Ah – a replica, a full size working replica – from the moment that was proposed, the project seems to have taken off, becoming a quite remarkable spontaneous community effort. And it is worth noting that the concept was far more unusual then than it would be now. Of the most important components only the 45 ft wooden hull was built elsewhere, by G. Thomson of Buckie. Local companies did the rest – the engine was built by John G. Kincaid & Co. Ltd, the boiler by Rankin & Blackmore Ltd, and the ship was engined and fitted out at Lithgows Ltd's yard. Some twenty five local firms are recorded as having helped.

It is perhaps symptomatic of subsequent changes in shipbuilding that as recently as 1962 it was possible to construct an accurate replica of a 150-year old steam boat in this way. Even the detailed design work on the engine, which today one would expect to be the province of a marine historian or archaeologist, was entrusted to Kincaid's chief draughtsman, Mr Andrew Mumford. He was helped in his task by survival of the original *Comet*'s engine in the Science Museum, London, which he closely inspected and measured before the replica was built. So the replica engine with its single vertical cylinder and side lever arrangement has the stamp of authenticity, even though some details could only be reconstructed from supposition. Because metal had become brittle, for instance, the museum authorities would not permit the cylinder or valve casing of the original engine to be opened for examination, and of its jet condenser only the cast iron box remained. Much less information was available about the original boiler; eventually a wagon-type boiler was built for a maximum steam pressure of 10 lb per sq. in. – the engine was to work, like the original, at 7 lb per sq. in. Following the best available information on the layout of the original boat, the boiler was positioned in the hull to port and the engine alongside it to starboard, driving two pairs of paddle wheels through spur gears. The funnel, twenty five feet high, doubled as a mast to support a square sail, and a jib could be carried on the forestay.

Official booklets published soon afterwards give the impression that the replica *Comet* was launched on 1 September 1962 and immediately moved off satisfactorily under her own steam. This performance seemed to the author quite remarkable, until when searching through a photographic record of the project, which now belongs to Norman Burniston Photography of Greenock, I found some negatives, carefully dated, which show the *Comet* being fitted out afloat in Lithgows Ltd's Kingston Basin on 27 August! It is a fair guess that some trials were quietly run before she was hauled out again.

Certainly the ceremonial naming ceremony and launching did take place at Lithgows Ltd's East Yard soon after 12.30 pm on 1 September. After lunch, and a mile-long procession of decorated floats through the town, the official party of fourteen notables, all dressed in early-nineteenth century costume, went aboard her at Kingston Basin. The replica *Comet* then voyaged to Helensburgh and back, satisfactorily if by modern standards slowly. Two hundred small craft gathered to accompany her: 15,000 people waited in the rain to welcome her on her return, after dark, to Port Glasgow.

Over the next two weeks, more than 7,000 people paid to visit the *Comet* in Kingston Basin. The Comet Trust Fund was set up to build a home for her and provide travelling scholarships for shipbuilding apprentices. But euphoria evaporates, and neither goal was to be achieved. The replica was, however, stored under cover until 1974 when she was loaned to the Burgh of Port Glasgow, which placed her on display on her present site, close to where the original was built.

In 1983 Inverclyde District Council, which had succeeded the Burgh of Port Glasgow, accepted the replica *Comet* from Scott Lithgow as a gift, together with the £2,800 remaining in the trust fund, to be used towards repairs. Repairs to the hull in fact cost considerably more than this; they

With steam to spare, replica paddle steamer *Comet* passes Greenock en route for
Helensburgh on 1 September 1962.　　　NORMAN BURNISTON PHOTOGRAPHY

had become necessary largely because the pond around the ship (the
fence is a later addition) had been insufficient to keep intruders from
going aboard to sleep in the cabins, and to use them as a lavatory. The
interior had to be cleaned and fumigated before repair work could start.

From the ground beside *Comet* one can see much of the hull and
paddles, but little of the machinery, and while I was preparing this book
the district council kindly arranged for me to go on board the vessel.
The machinery was still in place – it appeared substantially complete
and less vandalised than I had feared. Indeed although the pressure
gauge was broken and some of the insulating brickwork around the
boiler missing, the glass tube of the boiler water level gauge was still
intact. The actual condition of the boiler could not of course be established without a proper inspection, but there is little sign of wear about
the machinery, or the hull: the vessel saw little actual use, and gives the
impression they made a good job of her when they built her.

On deck, too, the significance of the replica's location becomes clear,
for one is sufficiently elevated to see over that high wall on the other
side of the dual carriageway, to the Clyde shimmering beyond, with
Helensburgh distant on the farther shore. In an ideal world a viewing
gallery would be provided to enable visitors to admire both the machinery, and the view. For the continued preservation of the vessel there are
thoughts of moving her under cover into a controlled environment, but
whether this is achieved or not, she is now being looked after better

than she was, and this seems likely to continue. There are, after all, only another twenty three years or so before further celebrations will be in order for the original *Comet*'s bicentenary.

*W*illiam Symington to my mind exercises the greatest fascination of all Scottish pioneers of steam. Symington was the most heroic of failures: he achieved technical success with his steam boat *Charlotte Dundas*, but commercial success eluded him because of circumstances beyond his control. He also left us a considerable enigma by concealing, in his own account of his experiments, the existence of an earlier version of his eventually successful boat: but that the *Charlotte Dundas* comprised not one but two successive boats is made quite clear in Harvey and Downs-Rose's biography, and I have suggested in my own *The Archaeology of the Transport Revolution* a possible reason for concealment of the first.

In that book I described Symington's work at length, and in contemporary context. His steam boat experiments fell into two groups. The first were carried out during 1788-9 under the patronage of Patrick Miller, banker and shareholder in the Forth & Clyde Canal which was then under construction, with the eastern part already open. These experiments involved first fitting an atmospheric engine into a boat on the loch at Dalswinton, Miller's country house near Dumfries; and then constructing a larger version which was operated on the Forth & Clyde Canal near Falkirk – but not sufficiently well to arouse the continuing enthusiasm of the patron, who withdrew, while it seems likely that its engine contravened the 'catch-all' patent on the separate condenser held by James Watt.

It was only in 1800, the year that Watt's patent expired, that Symington was invited by Lord Dundas, Governor of the Forth & Clyde Canal company, to develop a steam boat for towing vessels through the canal: and so Symington carried out his second series of experiments between 1800 and 1803. The result, the paddle tug *Charlotte Dundas* (named after his lordship's daughter) gave a convincing demonstration of her powers on 28 March 1803 when she towed two sloops for 19½ miles along the canal against a gale so strong that no horse-drawn vessel could move to windward at all. Yet she did not go into service: this was probably a consequence of jealousies within the canal's hierarchy of management. The excuse was that her wash might damage the banks. Earlier the great Duke of Bridgewater had ordered eight similar tugs for his Bridgewater Canal – but he had died on 8 March 1803 and the order was subsequently countermanded by the canal superintendent. Symington was denied the rewards of success. The steam plant was removed from *Charlotte Dundas* and her hull was eventually broken up in the early 1860s: some relics of her timbers survive in Grangemouth Museum.

Recent interest in Symington's work has prompted construction of replicas of two of his boats – the Dalswinton boat and the *Charlotte Dundas*. The original Dalswinton boat had twin hulls, with two paddle wheels mounted in line between them. Miller had been experimenting with manually-operated paddle wheels for moving ships independently of the wind. The engine, much restored, survives in the Science Museum, London. Symington used two vertical open-topped cylinders of atmospheric type, and converted reciprocating motion to rotary by means of chains, ratchets and pawls: application of the crank to steam engines had been patented by James Pickard in 1780. The boat was operated under steam on Dalswinton Loch in October 1788.

Construction of the replica was proposed in 1985 by David Landale, present owner of Dalswinton, to James Neil, principal of Dumfries & Galloway College of Technology, with a view to commemorating the bicentenary of the original vessel. A feasibility study then showed that the project would be practicable given Manpower Services Commission aid, both physical and financial. Design of this full-size replica was based on historical research and co-ordinated by T. Goldstraw of Elton Boatbuilding Co., Kirkcudbright. The eventual boat is 25 ft long overall by 7 ft beam; the hulls were clinker-built of larch on oak by an MSC team using timber provided by Dalswinton Estate. David Landale also, I understand, largely financed purchase of castings for the boat. Cylinder castings were machined by apprentices of NEI Thomson Cochran, Annan, who also made a dummy boiler and funnel, for this is a non-working replica, if only for safety reasons. Most of the rest of the machinery, including the paddle wheels, was made by the college of technology, and though the boiler is dummy, the engine is thought to be workable. The possibility has been considered of connecting an electric motor to it, in the event of the boat's being launched, with the alternative of fitting an outboard motor to the transom beam. The total cost of the vessel was some £150,000, and she was ready in time to be displayed at the Glasgow Garden Festival throughout the summer of 1988.

After the festival the boat was brought back to Dumfries, and placed on display at Dumfries & Galloway College of Technology pending a

decision on her eventual resting place. The decision to make this a non-working replica, though at first sight disappointing, is perhaps wise: the extent to which the original boat actually moved under steam has long been a matter of mild controversy, and although it undoubtedly did so, there is equally no doubt that the engine was underpowered for the boat: so the performance of a working replica might well be so poor as to be an anti-climax.


## R E P L I C A   C H A R L O T T E   D U N D A S

*T*he *Charlotte Dundas* of 1803 was the culmination of the work which Symington started at Dalswinton. Historians differ over the stages through which development went between 1800, when the second phase of his experiments started, and 1803, but there is no doubt that the engine of the final version had a horizontal double-acting cylinder driving direct on to a crankshaft. This arrangement, subsequently common in many steam engine applications except, paradoxically, marine, was Symington's original work. He patented it in 1801 at a period when the normal arrangement for a steam engine was a vertical cylinder with drive through an overhead beam. *Charlotte Dundas* had a single paddle wheel, set in a recess in the stern with twin rudders, one either side; probably at various stages the paddle wheel was mounted directly on the crankshaft, or driven through gears. She was built at Grangemouth, which was then developing around the eastern entrance to the Forth & Clyde Canal, and engine parts were supplied by the Carron Company.

Today Grangemouth, Falkirk, and the eastern end of the Forth & Clyde Canal all lie within Falkirk District. The canal was formally closed to navigation in 1963, but much of it, except in Grangemouth itself, remains in water: it is seeing increasing use by pleasure craft and there are hopes of restoration of the locks. By 1986 Falkirk District Council had a well-established Manpower Services Commission workshop for its Museums Service. Its achievements included restoration of a threshing mill and a Falkirk electric tram. Thoughts turned to the possibility of building a replica of Symington's 1789 boat for its bicentenary, but were soon modified into a decision to build instead a replica of his much more important *Charlotte Dundas.*

Replica of Miller's and Symington's Dalswinton steam boat was exhibited at the Glasgow Garden Festival during 1988.                    AUTHOR

Hull of replica *Charlotte Dundas* was built by Cockenzie Slip & Boatyard Ltd and launched on 4 November 1988, after which she was towed to Grangemouth for steam plant to be installed. AUTHOR

This, it was decided, would be a working replica, steam driven, with the intention that it would eventually operate on the canal, towing a passenger boat. Because the original boat was large – 66 ft long – and the channel of the canal is now restricted, it was decided to make the replica three-quarters full size. Even this has produced a boat some 50 ft long. The estimated cost was some £176,000, to be met by Falkirk D.C., the Manpower Services Commission, and sponsorship by local industries.

Construction of the wooden hull was put out to contract to Cockenzie Slip and Boatyard Ltd, of Cockenzie, East Lothian, a traditional boat-builder well able to undertake the task. Because *Charlotte Dundas* is flat-bottomed – the design was clearly derived from canal lighters of the time – the builder could not follow the usual practice of starting from the keel and working upwards: instead the frames of oak were built upside down, and the bottom planked with larch planks and caulked before the skeletal vessel was turned right way up. The main keel gives way to twin keels at the stern, one each side of the paddle-wheel recess. The completed hull was tried out afloat, hauled out and then ceremonially launched on 4 November 1988: Provost Goldie of Falkirk and Mrs Goldie turned out in period costume and Mrs Goldie performed the naming ceremony.

Once afloat, *Charlotte Dundas* was taken in tow by a Forth Ports Authority tug for the voyage up the Firth of Forth to Grangemouth. The day was, fortunately in view of the time of year, calm and clear, and *Charlotte Dundas* successfully reached the berth waiting for her, where her steam plant was to be installed. This at the time of the launch was already under construction. The cylinder, for instance, had been cast by Tayforth Foundry Ltd and was being machined by Daniel Industries Ltd, both of them Larbert firms. Many small components were being made in the museum service's own workshop. It was anticipated that the replica *Charlotte Dundas* would be completed during 1989.

# OPEN AIR AND
# OPERATING
# MUSEUMS

## THE GRAMPIAN TRANSPORT MUSEUM

*A*ndrew Lawson, Postie of Craigievar, Aberdeenshire, at the end of the last century, was a most remarkable man. The mail had to be collected from Whitehouse station, on the Great North of Scotland Railway's Alford branch: this meant a daily journey of about seven miles each way over indifferent roads, with all the extra mileage for individual deliveries in addition. The Post Office made him a small allowance for keeping a horse: Lawson, who had trained as a joiner before becoming postman, built himself a cart to carry the mail in fine weather, a covered van for foul, and a sledge for snow. In his spare time, which must have been very limited, he also did all the carpentry for constructing his own house, he set up a water wheel to drive a lathe and sawmill in his workshop, he added a dynamo to generate his own electricity, and he became a skilled photographer. His most remarkable achievement, however, was to design and build for himself a steam-driven horseless carriage. He did this in 1895, when it is unlikely that he personally had seen any steam road vehicle smaller than a traction engine.

Today this vehicle, which perhaps inevitably gained the name *Craigievar Express*, is the most prized exhibit at the Grampian Transport Museum. By happy coincidence this is located at Alford a few miles north of Craigievar. Here the *Craigievar Express* can be seen by the public, not only stationary in the museum, but also on special occasions in steam and running. It appears primitive: but it is less so than it appears. In 1895 design conventions for light self-propelled road vehicles were still at the formative stage. The *Craigievar Express* combines two well established technologies. The body and wheels are well-made of wood, as one would expect from a joiner (a couple of years later, in America, the Stanley Brothers would use bicycle-frame technology). The body is open, and on it are mounted a vertical boiler and a single-cylinder horizontal steam engine. Both were of established type and the engine is probably much older than the vehicle.

The *Craigievar Express* is a three-wheeler; the rear wheels are driven through a differential, remarkable for the period, and the front wheel is steerable. In choosing a three-wheeled layout, Lawson is thought to have been influenced by the work of Benz in Germany, which had been reported in the British technical press. How often Lawson actually used his vehicle to carry the mail is not clear, but a mail-bag sized luggage space ahead of the boiler suggests that what the designer set out to build was a steam-driven mail cart. Certainly, when the museum had the opportunity to buy the *Craigievar Express* a few years ago, the Scottish Postal Board joined the National Heritage Memorial Fund in assisting with finance.

The Grampian Transport Museum is operated by the Grampian Transport Museum Association. This voluntary association was founded in Aberdeen in 1978; it is a charity, and is at the time of writing seeking to transform itself into a company limited by guarantee. Grampian Region helped by making available some disused land next to the closed railway station at Alford, Aberdeenshire, and the region and the European Economic Community Regional Development Fund provided grants to restore the station building and build the exhibition hall. The buildings belong to the region; the museum in its present form opened in 1983.

The main exhibition hall contains an extensive collection of road vehicles, motor and horsedrawn as well as steam; the mellow tones of a 1923 Mortier dance organ fill the hall at intervals. Most of the exhibits are privately owned, displayed under loan agreements for limited periods, a scheme which leads to variety for returning visitors. Notable among the exhibits accompanying the *Craigievar Express* during 1988 was a Sentinel S4 steam wagon of 1935 – probably the ultimate development of the road steam goods vehicle. A vertical coal-fired boiler to the rear of the cab supplies steam to a four-cylinder engine driving the rear axle by shaft. This particular vehicle was operated by a distillery from 1936 until 1954 and is owned by William Teacher & Sons Ltd.

Outside the main building was displayed the large portable engine *Birkhall*, donated to the museum by HRH the Duke of Edinburgh. This was built by Marshall & Sons of Gainsborough as late as 1942 for the Ministry of Supply – one of a batch ordered at that time probably

Fowler traction engine is linked to threshing machine at Grampian Transport Museum on a steam activity Sunday, 26 June 1988.                    AUTHOR

because they could be fuelled on waste wood and sawdust rather than war-scarce oil. It powered a sawmill on the Balmoral estate until the 1970s; in 1988 an appeal was being made for funds to restore it to working order.

Perhaps the pleasantest feature of the Grampian Transport Museum is that it comprises not only a hall where its exhibits are displayed static, but also an outdoor demonstration area where they are displayed on the move. Activity Sundays are organised throughout the summer; in 1988, 26 June was steam power Sunday and several visiting traction engines, a steam roller and two miniature traction engines joined the *Craigievar Express* in action. For 1989 it is planned that the Bon-Accord Steam Engine Club will host an event on the last Sunday in June. The principal event of the year (23 July in 1989) is Alford Cavalcade, a rally of vintage vehicles of all types, including steam.

Railway exhibits appear in the Alford Valley Railway Museum, part of the Grampian Transport Museum but housed in the old railway station building. These are small exhibits, mostly of local interest. They include photographs, tickets, luggage labels, maps and other ephemera. The Grampian Transport Museum is open daily from the beginning of April until the end of September.

*M*any places in Scotland saw increasing industrial prosperity in the last century succeeded by depression in this, but few if any more so than Coatbridge, Lanarkshire. At the beginning of the last century it was a rural area: at its end, the principal iron-producing district of Scotland. Collapse of that industry in the present century left Coatbridge with an extreme problem of urban dereliction, and out of measures taken to alleviate it has come Summerlee, a large-scale open-air museum of social and industrial history with the emphasis – absent in any other Scottish museum – on heavy industry.

During the last century, Summerlee was one of Coatbridge's most important ironworks. It eventually ceased production in 1930; its site was used in the 1960s by a manufacturer of cranes which in turn went into liquidation in 1980, leaving Monklands District Council to inherit a large building in an area of near-derelict land.

It is this area which has become the main site for the working museum created by Summerlee Heritage Trust. The proposal originated in the early 1980s from Land Use Consultants – this firm had been retained by Monklands D.C. to advise on improvements, much needed, to the course of the Monkland Canal. The canal was laid out originally by James Watt, but by the 1980s had long been closed. One of the improvements was re-excavation, as an amenity, of a length of the canal's Gartsherrie branch (completed by 1982) adjacent to the site of Summerlee ironworks, and it is on either side of the canal that the heritage trust's museum is being laid out. The museum covers twenty five acres and is skirted along its eastern boundary by one of the few remaining sections of the pioneer Monkland & Kirkintilloch Railway which is still in operation: in 1831 the M & K was the first railway in Scotland to make regular use of steam locomotives.

Summerlee Heritage Trust is a charity and a company limited by guarantee with trustees drawn from district and regional councils and independent experts. Finance has come from Monklands District Council and the European Regional Development Fund among others; much of the work has been done through Manpower Services Commission schemes. After a preview season in 1987, Summerlee opened to the public in 1988.

Heavy industry in the last century meant steam power, and this is well represented among the trust's holdings. Perhaps the most notable is a Newcomen-type engine built in 1810 which operated at Farme Colliery,

Farme Colliery's Newcomen engine, dating from 1810, is displayed temporarily in the main exhibition hall at Summerlee, pending construction of an outdoor coal mine exhibit.                    SUMMERLEE HERITAGE TRUST

Marshall Fleming steam crane was restored to working order by Summerlee engineers in 1988, and is to be demonstrated regularly during 1989.

Rutherglen. Just why the atmospheric principle was used for an engine built at that late date is not clear, for Watt's patent restricting use of the separate condenser had expired ten years before. The engine seems to have been built largely by the colliery's own enginewright, so maybe it was simply a case of an old-fashioned man using a well-tried principle. At any rate he built soundly enough for the engine to run for over a century, being used seemingly both for pumping and winding. It is now on loan to Summerlee from Glasgow Museums; it has been on display (apparently for the first time since it was dismantled in 1915) in the main exhibition hall, but it was intended to re-erect it as part of an outdoor coal mining exhibit.

Summerlee has two rail-mounted steam cranes built by Marshall, Fleming & Co. Ltd. of Motherwell, one of which, a twin cylinder steel-works crane built in 1943 to a design from the 1880s, was restored to operation in 1988. The other is a high-speed six-cylinder crane on loan from the National Museums. Summerlee also has two railway locomotives: a Sentinel four-wheeled vertical boilered locomotive with geared drive, scheduled for restoration to running order soon, and a Hudswell Clark 0-6-0 tank locomotive which is a longer term project. One of the largest exhibits on display is a colliery winding engine built by local firm Murray & Pattison which ran at Cardowan Colliery, four miles from Sum-

Summerlee Heritage Trust's Fowler compound steam roller is to be seen at work by visitors.                    SUMMERLEE HERITAGE TRUST/TREVOR REES

merlee, until 1984. In store at present, and on loan from Glasgow Museums, is a large two-cylinder double beam engine.

Summerlee also features authentic historic workshops where belt-driven machine tools, including drills, lathes and planning machines, can be seen in use, repairing and manufacturing parts for restoration of working exhibits. It is hoped to provide this service also for other museums and preservation groups.

The museum intends to acquire a steam roller, which visitors will see at work, rolling roads around the site. Steam rollers and engines belonging to members of the Scottish Traction Engine Club can often be seen at Summerlee between rallies, and Summerlee itself hosts a steam fair at the end of August. During 1989 it is hoped to have something in steam every Wednesday and Sunday from May to September; the museum itself is open all the year except for a short period over the Christmas and New Year holiday. Other attractions at Summerlee include archaeological excavations of the 1830s ironworks, a working electric tramway, a working sawmill intended to open in 1989, and a full-size replica of the *Vulcan*, the first iron boat (horse-drawn) built in Scotland.

*A*t the former colliery at Preston-
grange, East Lothian, which is now part of the Scottish Mining Museum,
one can visit a beam engine in situ in its engine house. It is an opportunity unique in Scotland. The engine was installed to drain the mine in
1874: but it was not new then, for it was first built in 1853 and used in
Cornwall before it was dismantled by Harvey & Co. of Hayle and sent by
sea to Prestongrange.

At Prestongrange it is said to have operated continuously until 1954,
although there must have been pauses for instance when the beam had
to be strengthened to cope with the load from three pumps installed in
1905 at levels 210, 420 and 780 feet below the surface, and in 1916 and
1938 when a fractured piston rod damaged the cylinder. The colliery
closed in 1962 and most of its buildings were demolished (including,
presumably, the boilers) by the National Coal Board. By 1968 the beam
engine and its house were threatened with demolition too. Fortunately
the late David Spence, former manager of the colliery, took steps with
the then East Lothian County Council to have it preserved: eventually
the colliery site was acquired by the council and the beam engine scheduled as an ancient monument.

From this grew the idea of a museum of Scottish coal mining. David
Spence had assembled a small collection of coal mining relics, and in
1980 the coal board decided that the museum should be located at
Prestongrange. The local authority, by then East Lothian District Council, set Colin McLean to work on the plan for this, but in 1981 even while
he was doing so, Lady Victoria colliery at Newtongrange, Midlothian,
was scheduled for closure. This clearly had great potential for a mining
museum for, unlike Prestongrange, most of its buildings were still standing. The eventual outcome was that the Scottish Mining Museum Trust
(which was established in 1984 as a company limited by guarantee, and
a charity) has two sites, Lady Victoria and Prestongrange, and Colin
McLean is its director.

The Prestongrange engine house is open to the public (although it
may be necessary for intending visitors to ask in the museum reception
building for the engine house to be opened). The top of the pump rod
and part of the beam can in any event be seen from outside, for the fulcrum of the beam is supported, as was usual with beam engine houses,
by one of the walls. It is only at close quarters within, however, that the
sheer size of the thing becomes manifest. The single vertical cylinder
has a diameter of 70 inches and a stroke of 12 feet. Ascending to the first

floor one finds oneself level with the top of the cylinder, a further ascent to the top floor brings one to fulcrum level and the beam itself, 33 feet long, over 6 feet deep at the fulcrum, and weighing 30 tons. When this engine ran, an operating speed of $3\frac{1}{2}$ strokes a minute enabled it to lift 650 gallons of water a minute.

External exhibits at Prestongrange include steam locomotives, steam cranes and wagons of types once typical at collieries. Once a month (in 1988, on the first Sunday) members of the Prestongrange Society operate a steam locomotive over some 400 yards of track, with passengers travelling in a curious vehicle acquired from British Rail which had earlier converted it from parcels van to engineer's brake van. The locomotive in use during 1988 was a 0-4-2 tank locomotive of 1914, but this was due for inspection which would mean lifting the boiler from the frames, and it was anticipated that an Andrew Barclay 0-4-0 tank would be running in 1989. In the long term the society would like to restore one of the cranes, to demonstrate loading a wagon and shunting it with the locomotive. The locomotives belong to the mining museum, but are maintained and operated by the society.

A steam rally is held each year in mid-June; the 1988 two-day event attracted two steam rollers, a showman's road locomotive, a steam fire engine, a fairground organ and various other vehicles.

The other important piece of steam plant in the care of the Scottish Mining Museum is the winding engine at Lady Victoria Colliery. This was built by Grant Ritchie & Co. Ltd. of Kilmarnock and installed in 1894; it operated until the colliery closed in 1981, constantly winding the cages containing tubs, or hutches, of coal up the 1,650 feet deep shaft, lowering the empties, and at appropriate times raising and lowering the miners themselves.

The engine is large, a twin cylinder horizontal engine with cylinders of 42 inches diameter and 7 feet stroke. It exhausted to atmosphere and drew steam from a range of Lancashire boilers which still exist, though out of use and inacccessible by the public; two were last used to steam the engine in 1983. For demonstration purposes, an electric motor has been installed to turn the winding drum and through it the engine: this keeps its parts moving and lubricated, for it is regularly demonstrated to visitors, who also visit the pit-head itself.

Both Prestongrange and Lady Victoria are open daily except Mondays. Volunteer supporters join the Friends of the Scottish Mining Museum.

# *S TEAM  E N G I N E S  I N .*
# *O P E R A T I O N*

*B*y 1980, Glenruthven Weaving
Mill at Auchterarder in Perthshire was the last surviving factory in Scotland driven by a steam engine; and in that year full production ceased and the engine was taken out of service. The mill dated from 1877, and the engine was installed in 1916, in place of a less powerful one. It was not new, even when installed, but about forty years old.

The mill closed completely in 1981, and was bought in 1982 by Glendevon Construction, a building business headed by Douglas Ross. Ross had then no particular interest in steam, but wanted the weaving shed as workshops. But before long the decision to preserve the engine in working order as an industrial monument had been taken, and to this end the Auchterarder Heritage Centre Trust was incorporated in 1984: a guarantee company formed for charitable purposes with half a dozen members including Ross as chairman, James Wood who is Curator of Engineering and Industry at the Royal Museum of Scotland, Eric Cooper one of the founders of the Strathspey Railway and Geoff Hayes mechanical engineer and authority on stationary engines.

The engine itself is a fine horizontal tandem compound – that is to say, high and low pressure cylinders are in line, with a common piston rod. The stroke is thirty inches; precisely what the cylinder diameters may be is not known, for members of the trust, whose principle is that when something works well it's best left alone, have not yet needed to remove the cylinder covers. A single eccentric works the valves for both cylinders, and steam is condensed by a jet condenser. The engine is supplied with steam from a Cornish boiler, though a smaller and more economical boiler has been obtained and it is intended to instal this.

Several steam-up dates are arranged each summer – during 1988 they were two weekends in July, two in August and one in September. On the Saturdays, the engine was running by 2 pm, and earlier on the Sundays; it ran until about 5 pm. Formerly it drove the looms through belts: now it runs light. Nevertheless it provides an all-too-rare opportunity to see (and smell) an industrial stationary steam engine running under steam with its flywheel spinning, in authentic surroundings.

The engine can be seen out of steam any day the heritage centre is open, which in 1988 was from Easter to October, seven days a week. Adjoining the steam engine is an exhibition about weaving and the locality; the main weaving shed now houses the Great Scots exhibition and display. This is operated by Strathearn Developments Ltd which now owns the building and leases the engine and boiler rooms to the heritage trust at a nominal rent.

## BIGGAR GASWORKS MUSEUM

*B*iggar Gasworks was selected for preservation at a time when conversion to North Sea gas was making it clear that town gasworks would soon become things of the past. It closed in 1973. The last operating gasworks in Scotland was eventually, I understand, Millport which closed in 1981. By that time Biggar was already open to the public, and today functions as one of the museums in the National Museums of Scotland.

Its relevance here is that among its equipment was a vertical cross-tube boiler by Farrar of Newark. This is now used to supply steam to enable two stationary engines in the National Museums' collection to run, under steam, on summer Sunday afternoons – that is, between the beginning of July and the beginning of September. Both engines have gasworks connections. One is a single-cylinder horizontal slide valve engine made by G. Waller of Stroud, Gloucestershire in, probably, the 1920s; it formerly drove a circulating pump at Dunoon Gasworks. The other is an enclosed single-cylinder high-speed engine by Sissons of Gloucester, dating from 1939, from Galashiels Gasworks.

Also at Biggar, as a static exhibit, is a small 2 ft gauge 0-4-0 tank locomotive, built by Andrew Barclay in 1903 to fit a restricted loading gauge. It was used at Granton Gasworks where a 2 ft gauge internal rail system was used to transport coke and materials.

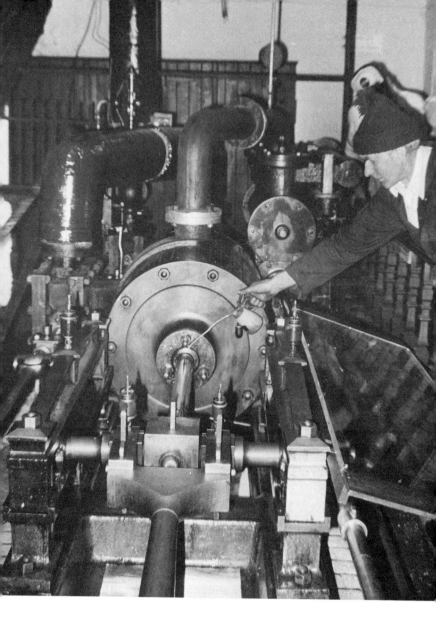

A drop of oil for Glenruthven Weaving Mill's tandem compound horizontal engine running under steam in 1988 at its original location, now part of Auchterarder Heritage Centre.

*A* steam-powered sawmill, it is intended, will be added in 1989 to the many attractions at the Landmark Highland Heritage & Adventure Park, Carrbridge, Inverness-shire. It will form part of a forestry heritage park, and the engine, a 12 hp Marshall portable built for the Ministry of Supply in the early 1940s, is already in position, under cover, at the time of writing late in 1988.

In the early 1970s this engine belonged to Mearns Sawmills, Laurencekirk, from which it was purchased by Willie Smith of Forfar, a steam engine owner with experience in the timber trade. This had included operating another engine of the same type, so that a spare piston was available to replace a damaged one in the Laurencekirk engine. The engine was eventually restored and taken to Carrbridge.

There Landmark intend to fire it with timber offcuts to power a working sawmill, with guards to protect the visiting public. It is anticipated that the sawmill will operate two or three times a week from May until the end of September; the Landmark heritage park itself is open every day.

## B I R K H I L L   C L A Y   M I N E

*A* steam engine formerly provided power at Birkhill Clay Mine, and a steam engine, it is proposed, will run there again. The mine and its buildings are being restored by Bo'ness Heritage Trust, as part of the trust's object of establishing a living museum of the industrial and social history of the Forth Valley, which will include also a 1920s village at Bo'ness. It is hoped to open the mine to the public in 1989; it adjoins to Birkhill station on the Bo'ness & Kinneil Railway which will provide the principal means of public access.

The mine formerly produced fireclay, which was last extracted in 1980. The fireclay was loaded into hutches running on a narrow gauge railway, which were hauled up a cable-worked incline to the mine buildings. There the fireclay, which had a consistency resembling coal, was milled to a state in which it could be moulded into firebricks and refractories. At one time steam was used to power both milling machinery and incline.

The engine which it is proposed to instal is a single cylinder horizontal engine, probably about 100 years old, with an 8 ft diameter flywheel. It was built by Mathers, a little-known Edinburgh maker. The intention is to locate it in the same engine house as the former engine, probably early in 1989, though completing the installation to enable it to run under steam will take longer. Eventually it is hoped to run it demonstrating some of the clay milling machinery.

Whether it could be arranged to operate the cable-hauled incline is another question, related to safety of the visiting public in the event of runaways or cable breakage. It would be nice if it could be done, though, for cable haulage by stationary steam engine is now, I believe, extinct in commercial use, although as a form of railway motive power it was once familiar and antedated the locomotive.

# *W*HAT
# *I*S
# *W*HERE?

*Beam Engines*
Royal Museum of Scotland; Scottish
Mining Museum, Prestongrange;
Summerlee Heritage Trust

*Locomotives, narrow gauge and
miniature*
Biggar Gasworks Museum, Bo'ness &
Kinneil Railway, Glasgow Museum of
Transport, Royal Museum of
Scotland, Springburn Museum
*see also* Steam Trains in Operation,
narrow gauge and miniature

*Locomotives, standard gauge*
Glasgow Museum of Transport,
Royal Museum of Scotland,
Summerlee Heritage Trust
*see also* Steam Trains in Operation,
standard gauge

*Marine steam engines*
McLean Museum & Art Gallery,
Scottish Maritime Museum
*see also* Steam Ships and Boats in
operation, and Steam Ships, static

*Models*
Glasgow Museum of Transport,
McLean Museum & Art Gallery,
Royal Museum of Scotland,
Springburn Museum

*Portable Engines*
Grampian Transport Museum,
Landmark Highland Heritage &
Adventure Park; Royal Museum of
Scotland

*Replica Ships and Boats*
*Charlotte Dundas*, Falkirk; *Comet*,
Port Glasgow; Dalswinton Steam
Boat, Dumfries

*Stationary Steam Engines*
Auchterarder Heritage Centre;
Biggar Gasworks Museum; Birkhill
Clay Mine; McLean Museum & Art
Gallery; Royal Museum of Scotland;
Scottish Maritime Museum; Scottish
Mining Museum, Lady Victoria
Colliery; Summerlee Heritage Trust

*Steam Cars*
Glasgow Museum of Transport,
Grampian Transport Museum, Royal
Museum of Scotland

*Steam Cranes*
Scottish Industrial Railway Centre;
Scottish Mining Museum,
Prestongrange; Summerlee Heritage
Trust

*Steam Fire Engines*
Glasgow Museum of Transport

*Steam Rollers*
Glasgow Museum of Transport,
Summerlee Heritage Trust

*Steam Ships and Boats in operation*
PS *Waverley,* SL *Lady Rowena,* SS
*Auld Reekie,* SS *Sir Walter Scott,* SS
*VIC 32*

*Steam Ships, static*
PS *Maid of the Loch,* Renfrew Ferry,
SY *Ocean Mist*

*Steam Trains in Operation, narrow
gauge and miniature*
Alford Valley Railway, House of Ross
Miniature Railway, Kerr's Miniature
Railway, Lochgilphead Miniature
Railway, Mull & West Highland
Narrow Gauge Railway, Strathaven
Miniature Railway

*Steam Trains in operation, standard
gauge*
Bo'ness & Kinneil Railway; British
Rail, Fort William-Mallaig and
elsewhere; Caledonian Railway
(Brechin) Ltd; Lochty Railway;
Scottish Industrial Railway Centre;
Scottish Mining Museum,
Prestongrange; Strathspey Railway

*Steam Wagons*
Glasgow Museum of Transport,
Grampian Transport Museum

*Traction Engines*
Glasgow Museum of Transport,
Grampian Transport Museum,
Summerlee Heritage Trust

*Turbines*
Royal Museum of Scotland, Scottish
Maritime Museum

# KEY TO STEAM LOCATIONS SHOWN ON GENERAL MAP

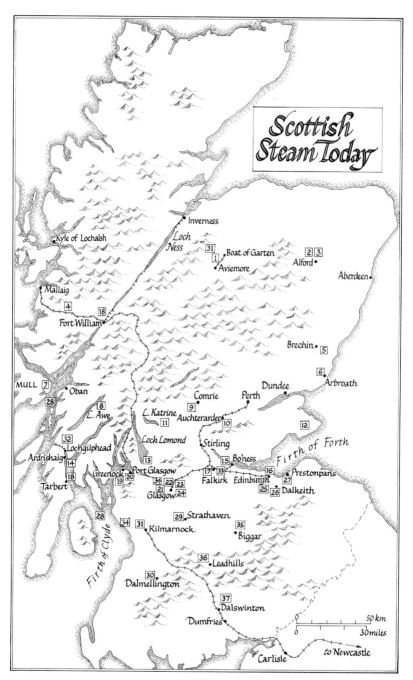

## Scottish Steam Today

- Inverness
- Kyle of Lochalsh
- Loch Ness
- [31] Boat of Garten
- [1] Aviemore
- [2] [3] Alford
- Aberdeen
- Mallaig
- [4]
- [18] Fort William
- Brechin [5]
- [6] Arbroath
- MULL [7]
- Oban [8]
- [28]
- L. Awe
- L. Katrine [11]
- Comrie
- [9]
- Auchterarder [10]
- Perth
- Dundee
- [12]
- [32] Lochgilphead
- Ardrishaig
- [14]
- [18] Tarbert
- Loch Lomond
- Stirling
- [15] Bo'ness
- [17] [33] [16] Prestonpans
- Edinburgh [27]
- [25] [26] Dalkeith
- Greenock [19]
- Port Glasgow [13]
- [20]
- [34] [22] [23]
- [21] [24]
- Glasgow
- Falkirk
- [28]
- [34] [31] Kilmarnock
- [29] Strathaven
- [35] Biggar
- Firth of Clyde
- [36] Leadhills
- [30] Dalmellington
- [37] Dalswinton
- Dumfries
- 50 km
- 30 miles
- to Newcastle
- Carlisle

— 137 —

# ADDRESSES, LOCATIONS
# &
# TELEPHONE NUMBERS

Addresses and telephone numbers are those for enquiries. Locations are at the same addresses, unless indicated otherwise. Page numbers for locations appear in the key to the general map on page 136.

Alford Valley Railway Co. Ltd, Main Street, Alford, Aberdeenshire. Principal station, Alford.

Auchterarder Heritage Centre Trust, Glenruthven Mill, Abbey Road, Auchterarder PH3 1DP; 07646 2079.

Ayrshire Railway Preservation Group: Hon. Secretary, Gordon Thomson, 4 Kyle Crescent, Loans, Troon, Ayrshire. Location, Scottish Industrial Railway Centre, Minnivey Colliery, Dalmellington, Ayrshire.

Biggar Gasworks Museum, see Royal Museum of Scotland for enquiries; location, Gasworks Road, Biggar, Lanarkshire.

Bo'ness & Kinneil Railway, Bo'ness Station, Union Street, Bo'ness, West Lothian, EH51 0AD; 0506 822298.

Bo'ness Heritage Trust, 86a North Street, Bo'ness, West Lothian, EH51 9NF; 0506 825855. Location, Birkhill Clay Mine, adjoining Birkhill Station, Bo'ness & Kinneil Railway.

Caledonian Railway (Brechin) Ltd, The Station, 2 Park Road, Brechin, Angus, DD9 7AF.

*Charlotte Dundas* replica: Curator of Museums, Falkirk District Council, Public Library, Hope Street, Falkirk FK1 5AU; 0324 24911. Replica under construction, location to be decided.

Dalswinton Steam Boat replica: The Principal, Dumfries & Galloway College of Technology, Heathhall, Dumfries, DG1 3QZ; 0387 61261.

Fort William-Mallaig steam trains: Information Centre, West Highland, ScotRail, Tom na Faire, Fort William; 0397 3791. Principal station, Fort William.

Glasgow Museum of Transport, 1 Bunhouse Road, Glasgow, G3 8DP; 041-357 3929.

Grampian Transport Museum, Alford, Aberdeenshire AB3 8AD; 0336 2292.

Kerr's Miniature Railway, West Links Park, Arbroath, Angus.

Landmark Highland Heritage and Adventure Park, Carrbridge, Aviemore, Inverness-shire; 047984 613.

Lochgilphead Miniature Railway: Bryan Passey, 19 McIntyre Terrace, Lochgilphead, Argyll. Temporary locations only – permanent line proposed.

Lochty Railway, Balbuthie, Leven, Fife; 03337 210. Principal station, Lochty, on B940 Crail-Cupar road.

Lowthers Railway Society Ltd: Mrs Jean Campbell, 23 Brora Crescent, Hamilton ML3 8LF. Principal station, Leadhills.

McLean Museum & Art Gallery, 9 Union Street, Greenock PA16 8JH; 0475 23741.

Mull & West Highland Narrow Gauge Railway Co. Ltd, Craignure (Old Pier) Station, Craignure, Isle of Mull, Argyll, PA65 6AY; 06802 494 (out-of-season telephone enquiries to 06803 389 or 472).

PS *Comet* replica: Director of Recreational Services, Inverclyde District Council, Municipal Buildings, Greenock PA15 1LQ; 0475 24400. Location, Port Glasgow (see text).

PS *Maid of the Loch,* MV *Countess Fiona* (on Loch Lomond): Maid of the Loch Ltd, Balloch Pier Road, Balloch, Dunbartonshire; 0389 52044. *Countess Fiona* only operating – principal departure point, Balloch Pier.

PS *Waverley:* Waverley Excursions Ltd, 36 Anderston Quay, Glasgow G3 8HA; 041-221 8152. Routes various, see text.

Paddle Steamer Preservation Society, see PS *Waverley*

Renfrew Ferry Museum: Chief Curator of Museums & Art Galleries, Renfrew District Council, High Street, Paisley PA1 2BA; 041-889 3151. Location to be decided.

Royal Museum of Scotland, Chambers Street, Edinburgh, EH1 1JF; 031-225 7534

SL *Lady Rowena* (on Loch Awe): Dalriada Steam Packet Co. Ltd, 9 Weymouth Drive, Glasgow G12 0LX; telephone Dalmally (08382) 440 during operating hours in season, otherwise 041-334 2529. Principal departure point, Loch Awe Station Pier, off A85 Tyndrum-Oban road.

SS *VIC 32*, The Change House, Crinan Ferry, Lochgilphead, Argyll, PA31 8QH; 05465 232. Routes various, see text.

SS *Sir Walter Scott* (on Loch Katrine): Strathclyde Regional Council Water Department, Loch Katrine Area, 419 Balmore Road, Glasgow G22 6NU; 041-336 5333, ask for 'steamer enquiries'. Principal departure point, Trossachs Pier.

SY *Ocean Mist* restaurant: Leith Steamship Company, 14 The Shore, Leith, Edinburgh EH6 6QW; 031-553 7627.

Scottish Industrial Railway Centre, see Ayrshire Railway Preservation Group.

Scottish Maritime Museum, Laird Forge Building, Gottries Road, Irvine, Ayrshire, KA12 8QE; 0294 78283.

Scottish Mining Museum, Lady
Victoria Colliery, Newtongrange,
Midlothian, EH22 4QN; 031-663
7519 (located also at Prestongrange,
adjacent B1348 Prestonpans-
Musselburgh Road).

Scottish Railway Preservation
Society, see Bo'ness & Kinneil
Railway.

Springburn Museum, Atlas Square,
Ayr Street, Glasgow G21 4BW; 041-
557 1405.

Strathspey Railway Co. Ltd, The
Station, Boat of Garten, Inverness-
shire, PH24 3BH; Boat of Garten
692.

Summerlee Heritage Trust, West
Canal Street, Coatbridge ML5 1QD;
0236 31261.

# FURTHER READING

Butcher, A.C., (editor), *Railways Restored*, Ian Allan Ltd, London, 1988 (re-issued annually)

Davison, C.St.C.B., *History of Steam Road Vehicles*, H.M.S.O., London, 1970

Deith, C.L., *Steam Heritage Yearbook 1988/9*, TEE Publishing, Hinckley, 1988 (re-issued annually)

Harvey, D.W., *A Manual of Steam Locomotive Restoration and Preservation*, David & Charles, Newton Abbot, 1980

Harvey, W.S., and Downs-Rose, G., *William Symington, Inventor and Engine Builder*, Northgate Publishing Co. Ltd, 1980

Hayes, G., *Stationary Steam Engines*, Shire Publications Ltd, Aylesbury, 1987

Hillsdon, B.E., and Smith, B.W., (editors) *Steamboats and Steamships of the British Isles*, Steam Boat Association of Great Britain, 72 Marlborough Road, Ashford, Middlesex, 1988

Macleod, I., and Neil, J., *The Dalswinton Steamboat 1788 – 1988*, T.C. Farries & Co. Ltd, Dumfries, 1988

*Museums in Scotland*, H.M.S.O., London, 1986

Nicholson, M., and O'Neill, M., *Glasgow Locomotive Builder to the World*, Polygon Books, Edinburgh, 1987

Ransom, P.J.G., *The Archaeology of the Transport Revolution, 1750 – 1850*, World's Work Ltd, Tadworth, 1984

Rowland, K.T., *Steam at Sea*, David & Charles, Newton Abbot, 1970

*The Comet*, Port Glasgow Town Council, Port Glasgow, 1962

van Riemsdijk, J.T., and Brown, K., *The Pictorial History of Steam Power*, Octopus Books Ltd, London, 1980

Many of the principal museums, societies etc mentioned in the text produce guide books or catalogues to their collections.

# *Acknowledgements*

I am greatly indebted to the following for their assistance in providing information for this book:

Mrs Catherine Barclay, Douglas Barclay, Bill Barrack, Chris Barry, Brian Bathgate, John Beveridge, Valerie Boa, Norman Brown, Tim Brown, Douglas Buchan, John Burnie, Norman Burniston, John B. Cameron, David Carnduff, G.J. Cassidy, John Clayson, Eric Cooper, Mrs E. Craig, J.A. Douglas, Graham Ellis, Robert Forsythe, D. Fullerton, Dr Ann Glen, James Gordon, Andrew Harper, David Hayes, Geoff Hayes, John Hutchinson, A. Ireland, Bob Kass, Stephen Kay, Andrew Kennedy, Matthew B. Kerr, F.R. Khan, Jim Lennox, Dr Joe McKendrick, John Mackenzie, Colin McLean, John Malden, D.I. Morgan, Fred Multon, D.L. Neill, Mike Oliver, Peter Ovenstone, M. O'Neill, Bryan Passey, D.C. Rochester, Douglas Ross, J.M. Sanderson, Sandra Scott, Stuart Sellar, W. Roger Shaw, John Sheridan, David Stirling, Andrew R. Smith, Bob Smith, Willie Smith, Gordon Thomson, Nick Walker, M.J. Ward, Harry Watson, Terry Willington, James L. Wood, Charles Young;

and to my family for their patience.

The fire is thrown out at the end of the day's operations, Bo'ness.   AUTHOR